Everyday Ethics

Everyday Ethics

Brian Huss

broadview press

BROADVIEW PRESS
Peterborough, Ontario, Canada

Founded in 1985, Broadview Press is a fully independent academic publishing house owned by approximately twenty-five shareholders—almost all of whom are either Broadview employees or Broadview authors. Broadview is supported by a collaboration with Trent University, a liberal arts university located in Peterborough, Ontario—the city where Broadview was founded and continues to operate. Broadview is committed to environmentally responsible publishing and fair business practices.

Library and Archives Canada Cataloguing in Publication

Title: Everyday ethics / Brian Huss.
Names: Huss, Brian, author.
Identifiers: Canadiana (print) 20240465024 | Canadiana (ebook) 20240465032 | ISBN 9781554816101 (softcover) | ISBN 9781460408582 (EPUB) | ISBN 9781770489349 (PDF)
Subjects: LCSH: Ethics. | LCSH: Ethics—Textbooks. | LCGFT: Textbooks.
Classification: LCC BJ1012 .H89 2024 | DDC 170—dc23

Broadview Press handles its own distribution in Canada and the United States:
PO Box 1243, Peterborough, Ontario K9J 7H5, Canada
555 Riverwalk Parkway, Tonawanda, NY 14150, USA
Tel: (705) 482–5915
email: customerservice@broadviewpress.com

Canada

Broadview Press acknowledges the financial support of the Government of Canada for our publishing activities.

Edited by Robert M. Martin
Book design by Michel Vrana

Broadview Press® is the registered trademark of Broadview Press Inc.

PRINTED IN CANADA

For Poppy,
who regularly reminds me that
philosophy begins in wonder.

Contents

V. Children: Is it ok to ...

VI. Self-Care: Is it ok to ...

VII. Taboos: Is it ok to ...

VIII. Identity Issues: Is it ok to ...

Acknowledgments

Many people have helped me to write this text. Of particular help were the many colleagues and students who gave me ideas for topics. I stupidly did not keep track of who suggested which topic. Sorry about that. But if any of you are reading this and recognize one of your ideas, I thank you. Thanks to my students over the years at York University, who gave me feedback on several of the essays included here, and who are the inspiration for the whole book. Thanks too to Robert Martin for many useful suggestions, Christine Handley and Stephen Latta at Broadview Press, as well as four anonymous reviewers for Broadview (especially Reviewer #4: you are wonderful, whoever you are). A very special thanks is owed to Kristin Andrews for all of her help and support. Finally, for lots of help that came in various forms, I thank Jacob Beck, Alissa Centivany, Shereen Chang, David Curry, Denise Curry, Christopher Eliot, Alexandra Huss, Eric Huss, Marilyn Huss, Raymond Huss, Monika Jankowiak, Muhammad Ali Khalidi, Kevin Lande, Whitney Lilly, Alice MacLachlan, Mysti Murphy, Timothy Murphy, Robert Myers, and Claudine Verheggen.

Introduction

This book is meant to provide a way to think about ethics. The idea is to think about the moral aspects of situations that the average person is likely to encounter often, or at least from time to time. These everyday ethical issues are different from issues such as abortion, euthanasia, and capital punishment. It is important to discuss and think carefully about these big important topics, but for the most part we must try to reach verdicts about them in large groups; we must decide, as an entire society, what we are going to say or do about reproductive rights, the right to die, and punishment. Everyday ethical issues, on the other hand, are issues that force *individuals* to make ethical decisions.

There is a sense in which this book is *not* about ethics itself. As you surely know already, ethics is a huge, complex field. The essays in this book kinda ignore the complexity for the sake of quickly giving you something to think about. But the complex, difficult stuff is really important. In the essays that follow, ethical theories (e.g., consequentialism, deontology, virtue ethics) are usually not explicitly mentioned, even though some arguments clearly rely on aspects of various theories. Likewise, the question of what an ethical theory is supposed to be in the first place, the importance of consistency in ethical verdicts, deductive validity, the nature of inductive arguments, the rules of rational debate, the relevant fallacies and heuristics and biases, and much else, are not covered here, even though they are of the utmost importance. Again, this book is designed to get you fired up and ready to go, and not to be a comprehensive treatment of an entire area of study.

This book covers 40 everyday ethics topics. They are grouped by broad theme, but you can skip straight to any chapter and read it without first reading the chapters that come before. Each topic is presented as a question of the form, "Is it ok to _____?" When we ask whether it is "ok," what we're asking is whether it is morally permissible to do whatever goes in the blank. For each topic there is a clarification section that makes the question more specific or otherwise refines the question, and generally indicates what is and what is not being asked. Following the clarification section is a pro essay and a con essay. The pro essay answers the question with a "yes" and the con essay answers the question with a "no." Sometimes the pro essay is presented first, sometimes the con essay. Sometimes one of the essays will directly respond to the arguments made in the other, and sometimes the pro and con essays present arguments without acknowledging the arguments made in the other. For a few of the topics there is also an "Option 3" essay, in which it is suggested that either the positions or the arguments presented in both the pro and con essays are mistaken. As for the arguments themselves, I have tried to include a variety of different kinds of arguments as well as a variety of different ways of presenting them. (See the table that follows this introduction.) I happen to think that some of the arguments presented in what follows are pretty good arguments. I think that others are awful. Many of them probably need to be expanded, but one of my aims is to offer very short essays and to leave it to you to figure out how the arguments might be improved upon or criticized.

I would very much like to get feedback from readers. If there is an everyday ethics issue that is not covered here and which you think would be a good one to examine, I'd love to hear about it. In general, I'm interested to hear brutally honest appraisals and criticisms. You can reach me at huss@yorku.ca

Guide to Essays

Guide to Essays

Is it okay to ...

are both the pro and the con essay very short?	does one of the essays directly address the argument made in the other?	is an alternative to the pro and con positions (a third option) offered?	are standard form arguments presented?	is a major ethical theory at least alluded to?	is scientific research of obvious importance?
★	★				
★	★			★	★
★	★				★
	★				★
	★			★	
	★			★	
★		★			
	★			★	
				★	
	★			★	★
	★				
	★			★	
			★		
	★		★		
★			★	★	
				★	
★	★			★	
				★	★
	★			★	★

Guide to Essays

Is it okay to ...

are both the pro and the con essay very short?	does one of the essays directly address the argument made in the other?	is an alternative to the pro and con positions (a third option) offered?	are standard form arguments presented?	is a major ethical theory at least alluded to?	is scientific research of obvious importance?
	★		★		
★		★	★		
	★			★	
	★				
	★			★	
			★		
★					
				★	★
	★		★		★
	★				★
	★			★	
★		★	★		
★	★				
★			★		
					★
			★		
					★
	★				★
	★		★	★	★
	★	★			

I. The Public Sphere

Is it ok to ...

1. Is it ok to ride a crowded elevator one floor?

Clarification

Assume that the elevator is in a tall building—say 20 or more stories. Assume that the elevator is packed with people who want to go several floors up or down. Assume that a set of stairs is close by and easily accessible. Assume that the would-be one-floor rider is able-bodied and not carrying a heavy load. Is it morally permissible for the rider to get on at the first floor and get off at the second?

Pro

Of course it's permissible to take the elevator one floor. Everyone has an equal right to use the elevator, and you have that right whether you're taking the elevator one floor or seventeen. Furthermore, even if many people in the elevator are delayed by the one-floor rider, they won't be delayed for very long—maybe ten seconds. Anyone who is annoyed at being delayed ten seconds because of the reasonable actions of another person needs to (a) realize that they live in a society, which is supposed to be a cooperative endeavor, and (b) reevaluate their priorities. The individual who is annoyed by a ten-second delay to their daily routine is someone who gets annoyed way too easily. Here's one of the lessons: Just because someone's actions irritate you, that doesn't mean that they have done anything *wrong*. Maybe *you* are at fault for being irritated in the first place. Given the very minimal inconvenience involved in the elevator case, we should say that the one-floor rider is just fine and that anyone on the elevator who is bothered needs to learn to relax.

Con

Most of the possible moral transgressions discussed in this book are not terribly evil. Nobody would compare riding a crowded elevator one floor with murder. The *severity* of the wrongness is not the issue here. Rather, the issue is whether there is *anything* wrong with riding the elevator one floor. And there is. When you could easily take the stairs but instead inconvenience many other people, you're putting the well-being of one person—you—above the well-being of many. It is almost always wrong to place more importance on one person's well-being than on the well-being of many, and when that one person is the one who acts, that person's actions are also selfish. To ride a crowded elevator one floor is to announce to your fellow humans that you just don't care about them that much. Either you have given the matter some thought and have decided that you're more important than everyone else, or you have never even thought about the way your actions might inconvenience others. It's hard to say which is worse.

But what about the idea that everyone has an equal right to use the elevator? The problem with this defense is that it relies on a bizarre notion of what a right is. First, note that the whole question just is whether everyone—including the one-floor rider—has an equal right to ride the elevator. My claim is that it is false that everyone has the right, and I have argued for this claim. Hence just saying, "But everyone has an equal right to use the elevator" is very much like saying "Nuh-uh!" or "You're wrong," and that's not an argument. Second, saying that you have a *right* to something as trivial as riding an elevator makes a mockery of the whole idea of rights. Let's see, I have the right to life, the right to autonomy, and ... the right to ride an elevator. Saying that you have a right to ride an elevator is like saying that you have a right to a good hair day. If talk of rights is to make any sense at all, and if rights are to be morally relevant, then they have to be special. There's not much difference between thinking you have a right to just about everything and thinking you have no rights at all. The whole point of rights is that certain things are special and *must* be protected because they are more important than other things, which are not so special. Once people claim the right to ride an elevator, the distinction between the important things and the not-so-important things is lost. So, no, you don't have a right to ride an elevator. Furthermore, the one-floor rider needlessly inconveniences others. Pretty clearly, then, the one-floor rider acts immorally.

2. Is it ok to wait to merge when two lanes of traffic are reduced to one?

Clarification

The scenario is this: Construction work is being done on a major multi-lane highway, forcing one lane to be closed for some distance. Many signs indicating the lane closure are placed well ahead of the merger from two lanes to one. Is it morally permissible to drive down the soon-to-close lane until the merger is necessary and only then merge into the through lane?

Con

It is not morally permissible to wait until the last possible moment to merge. If you zip up the empty lane, you're passing cars and people who are waiting their turn to make their way through the construction zone. If you do not line up behind them, presumably it is because you want to make it through the zone before them. But you're not morally special. Why should you get to your destination any faster than anyone else? Those who have lined up in the through lane are delayed because of the lane closure. Those who speed down the other lane think that they shouldn't be delayed, even though they have arrived on the scene after those who are waiting their turn in line. Again, it is obvious that those who wait until the last moment to merge are not more important than everyone else. Yet, when they zoom down the empty lane, they're treating themselves as if they were more important. It is never moral to treat yourself as if you were more important than other persons. Therefore, zooming down the empty lane and merging at the last moment is immoral.

Pro

The problem with the claim that it is always immoral to wait to merge is that it assumes a certain mindset of those who do so. Yes, if you wait to merge because you want to get by quickly and don't care about others, then your actions are immoral. But what if your reason for merging late isn't selfish?

There is good reason to think that the most efficient use of the roadway is for both lanes of traffic to continue in their lanes as usual and then to use the zipper method at the point of the lane closure: one car from the left lane goes through, then one from the right, one from the left again, etc. I do not have room here to summarize the scientific evidence which suggests that waiting to merge and then using the zipper method moves more cars through the construction zone more quickly than the alternative, but trust me it does. (Or don't trust me. Look it up.)

If I wait to merge because I know that the zipper method would work best, then it seems like I'm following something very much like the Golden Rule: I'm doing as I would like others to do. I, like everyone else, would like to be delayed as little as possible. If we all used the zipper method, then we would all be delayed as little as possible. I wish *everyone* would stay in their lanes and then zipper their way into the one-lane section. It's hard to see how I act immorally if I act as I want everyone else to act. An important moral lesson here is this: One and the same behavior can be moral if your intentions are good but immoral if your intentions are bad. Again, I agree that the jerk who zooms down the empty lane because they think they're more important than everyone else acts immorally. But the informed driver who does the same thing not because they are selfish but because they are trying to follow the Golden Rule does not act immorally. If you wait to merge and if you do so *for the right reasons*, then that's ok.

3. Is it ok to let your lawn grow wild or to otherwise have an unkempt lawn or garden?

Clarification

We are not talking about a situation where there might be health or safety concerns. Neither are we talking about the possibility of breaking bylaws of various sorts. If it were illegal to let the grass in your lawn grow wild, then doing that would be wrong where you live. That's not what we are talking about. Imagine the property owner who legally keeps a lawn full of bare spots, dandelions, unraked leaves, who waits a long time between lawn mowings, makes no real attempt at landscaping, and keeps miscellaneous junk in their garden.

Pro

There are three main reasons why it is morally permissible for you to let your lawn grow wild. The first is simply that you own it and you should be able to do whatever you want with your own property as long as you don't hurt anyone. (Even if you don't own the property because you rent the house you live in, if you are the person responsible for maintaining the property, it seems like you should be able to maintain it however you see fit.)

The second reason is that, morally speaking, it doesn't really matter if other people don't like the look of your lawn or garden. I happen not to like the look of the typical well-maintained lawn that you might find in an upper-middle class area of the suburbs, but I don't think there is anything *immoral* about keeping such a lawn, as long as it is done in an environmentally responsible way. There is a difference between aesthetics and ethics. If the hippy is expected to tolerate their neighbor's attempt to recreate the Kew Gardens in miniature, then the neighbor should be expected to tolerate the hippy's weeds. Maybe the hippy has better things to do. Maybe they think that spending lots of time and money on their lawn would be a waste. After all, maintaining a magazine-quality lawn probably doesn't pass the deathbed test: When you're about to die and you're looking back on your life, are you going to be happy that you always had an impeccably manicured lawn? Even if the answer is yes, you shouldn't have any *moral* problem with the person who answers no.

The third reason why it is ok to let your lawn go wild has already been alluded to: a wild garden is much more likely to be environmentally beneficial than a pristine, monocultured lawn. So, for environmental reasons, the question should really be whether it is morally permissible *not* to let your lawn grow wild.

Con

There are two main reasons why it is morally impermissible to let your lawn grow wild, but before we get to those reasons, it is important to note that a *well-kept* lawn or garden need not cause any environmental harm. There is a difference between making your lawn look like a fancy golf course by growing only perfect Bermudagrass and maintaining a diverse collection of attractive, native plants. It is true that the former is morally problematic for environmental reasons, but the question at hand is whether the fact that a lawn or garden is unkempt makes it morally worse.

The first reason why it is not ok to let your lawn grow wild is just that there is a societal expectation that you will keep a decently maintained lawn, and societal expectations create moral requirements. Maybe letting your lawn grow wild doesn't immediately *harm* anyone, but neither does going to the grocery store in the nude. Would *that* be ok?

The second reason is that there is no obvious distinction between aesthetics and ethics, contrary to what is claimed in the pro essay. Just as there are objective facts about what is morally right and what is morally wrong, there are objective facts about what is beautiful and what is ugly. Furthermore, great beauty is a form of moral goodness and great ugliness is a form of moral badness. Hideous things are quite literally moral affronts. I'm not suggesting that letting your lawn grow wild is on a par with armed robbery, but it really is morally wrong to foster ugliness. Ugliness makes the world a worse place, and it can never be ok to make the world a worse place. An unkempt lawn is ugly and therefore it is not ok to let your lawn grow wild.

4. Is it ok to not call strangers on their moral transgressions?

Clarification

You often encounter strangers acting immorally. There's the jerk who cuts in line, the dolt who cuts their toenails on the subway, and the jackass who parks in a disabled parking spot, among many others. All of these actions are immoral, at least according to me. The question is whether it is morally permissible for you to do and say nothing about these transgressions. I would think that it is certainly morally permissible for you to do or say something, but are you morally *required* to do or say something about this kind of behavior?

Con

You are required to both inform people when they're doing something wrong (on the off chance that they don't already know) and also let them know that their bad behavior should stop. First, ask yourself why you don't say anything in these situations. Isn't the answer just that you are a bit of a coward? Isn't the real answer that you simply want to avoid the conflict involved in calling an asshole an asshole? If so, then note that the prospect of feeling uncomfortable is not a good excuse for not doing your moral duty. Being moral can be difficult and unpleasant. Again, the difficulty and unpleasantness are not all that relevant. If you have a moral duty to call people on their bad behavior, then the fact that it's not going to be a fun thing to do doesn't change the fact that you have the moral duty to do it. Similarly, it doesn't matter if other people who are in a position to say something don't. Just as unpleasantness doesn't get you out of your moral obligations, other people's lack of moral courage doesn't get you out of your obligation to say something to the wrongdoer.

The reason you have a moral obligation to say something to the wrongdoer is that social sanction is likely the only thing that might change their behavior. Consider the line cutter. They know what they're doing, and that it's forbidden. They know that they are treating other people as if they don't matter. I can only conclude that the line cutter knows that what they're doing is morally wrong. And yet they do it. They don't care. They're incredibly selfish. The line cutter seems to be someone who is perfectly willing to do immoral things, as long as they think they can get away with it. How, then, can we prevent them from doing these immoral things? The answer is that we don't let them get away with it. Imagine what would happen if every time someone tried to cut in a long line, *everyone* in the line were to complain loudly and tell that person to get to the back of the line. That kind of social pressure would have an effect. The line cutter would be likely to (a) get to the back of the line and (b) think twice about cutting in line in the future. Again, the line cutter is not the kind of person who does things because they are the right thing to do; it's pretty clear that they don't care about acting morally. That's unfortunate, but it's not like the rest of us just have to accept it. We can and should modify their behavior by strongly condemning their line cutting. If all of us should do it, then you should do it, even if others don't and even if you acting alone isn't as effective as everyone acting together.

Pro

Although it is certainly permissible for you to say something to a bad actor, you are not morally obligated to do so. Ironically, the reason has already been alluded to in the con essay. People who act immorally are not very likely to respond well to your verbal condemnation of their behavior. If someone is the kind of person who will cut in a long line, then they are also the kind of person who will react badly when you tell them that they shouldn't cut in line. Furthermore, they are also the kind of person who will continue to act selfishly whenever they have the opportunity. What this means is that if you say something to them, not only will you not have any positive effect, but you will also have to endure a confrontation with a jerk. Saying something to the jerk is likely to be bad all around. When you encounter a jerk flouting moral rules, you are in a lose-lose situation. In lose-lose situations, you cannot be morally required to do anything at all. You are not required *not* to say something, but you are not morally required to say something either.

Here is a little (true) story to illustrate the ineffectiveness of calling strangers on their moral transgressions. I was walking through the parking lot of a grocery store I was about to enter. The parking lot was busy. A car was pulling out of a spot. Another car was waiting, with its turn signal on. The driver was obviously signaling that he was going to take the parking space. Just as the first car backed out of the space, another car came from the other direction and quickly took the open spot. When the driver of this car exited her vehicle, so did the driver who was waiting for the spot. He told the spot stealer that she shouldn't do that. There might have been some cursing and name-calling involved. Other people, including me, joined in to chastise the spot-stealer. This "person" reacted this way, "You're not the police. You can't do anything to me." She then marched into the store. I was seething; I think the other people who witnessed this event were pretty upset too. The asshole who stole the spot didn't seem to be bothered. So what did saying something to her accomplish? I find it hard to imagine that the asshole refrained from stealing parking spots subsequently. She is probably out there right now, stealing someone's parking spot, or cutting her toenails on the subway, or torturing puppies. The rest of us felt angry, and anger is not a pleasant thing to feel. The consequences were all-around bad because we tried to call someone on her immoral behavior. Arguably, the world would have been a better place if the driver whose spot was stolen had just said to himself "Oh well" and found another spot.

Now, this is just one story, but there is reason to think that it is likely to be representative of what happens when you chastise a stranger. That reason is that the stranger has already proven themself to be an immoral jerk. Moreover, immoral jerks aren't usually too sensitive to social sanction. Since they know that other people don't like what they do, but they do it anyway, it seems they already don't care how others respond to their immoral behavior. That's what selfish people are like. Not caring about others is both a cause and an effect of selfishness. There is no winning when you encounter a selfish jerk, and that is why it is morally permissible for you to do nothing when you see a selfish jerk doing selfish, jerky things.

5. Is it ok to not vote?

Clarification

If someone is well-informed about politics and public policy and has opinions about which candidates in an election are best suited to a political office, is it morally permissible for them to just not vote? Let's restrict ourselves to large-scale elections to public office. We're not talking about voting in primaries or voting for the leader or representative of a small group. Think of national, state, or provincial elections.

Pro

Of course it is permissible to refrain from voting. The reason is simple: It only makes sense to vote if there is a reasonable chance that your one vote will make the difference in the election. Not only is there *not* a reasonable chance that your vote will make the difference, it is almost *certain* that your one vote won't make the difference. For this reason, voting doesn't make any sense. The whole purpose of your individual act of casting a ballot is to get your favored candidate elected, but you casting a ballot just isn't going to make any difference as to whether your candidate gets elected. So, voting doesn't serve its intended purpose and it doesn't make any sense to vote—there's no reason to vote. Obviously, if an action doesn't make any sense, then you are not morally obligated to do it. Therefore, you are not morally obligated to vote.

There are two common objections to this line of reasoning, and they're both bad objections. The first is to say that your one vote *might* make the difference in an election. Sure, it might, but the odds are infinitesimally small. (Seriously, do the math for any large election. There is a much, much greater chance that you will be eaten by a shark today.) I *might* win the lottery, but it would be a very bad idea for me to act as if I *will*. Similarly, your one vote might make the difference, but it makes no sense to act as if it will.

The second objection usually takes the form of a question: "But what if everyone thought that way?" or "But what if nobody voted?" This is a bizarre question, but if we are to take it seriously, then the answer is obvious—it's that if *nobody* else voted, then it *would* make a lot of sense for you to vote, because then your one vote would make the difference for sure. But you know that lots and lots of people are going to vote, so the question is asking you to imagine a world that is nothing like the world you actually live in. It's hard to see what the point even is of asking the question. It reminds me of a question asked by Will Ferrell when he was impersonating Harry Caray on *Saturday Night Live*: "If you were a hot dog and you were starving, would you eat yourself?"

Con

There is a point behind the question "But what if nobody voted?" and the point serves as an explanation for why you have a moral obligation not only to vote, but also to inform yourself about public policy and to think carefully about political issues so that you can vote responsibly. The point behind the question is that you have a moral obligation to act as you would want others to act. When you leave it to others to do what must be done by a large portion of the population, you are a free rider. You're no better than citizens who cheat on their taxes or don't pay their fare on public transit. As an adult member of a democratic society, you have a responsibility to help maintain democratic institutions and hence you have, *at the very least*, the responsibility to inform yourself on the issues and vote.

Your obligation to vote is not an obligation to any particular person, but rather to all of your fellow citizens. Your obligation to vote is not an obligation to get your favored candidate elected, but rather to contribute to the democratic process. To see this, imagine that you take a course in which you are put into a large group with others and the group must submit a project for a large percentage of each group member's grade. Even if your role in the group is minimal (because there are so many group members) and even if you know that the vast majority of the other group members will do what they're supposed to do, it would be wrong for you not to do your part. Your responsibility is not to group-member Nancy or to group-member Yoshi, but rather to the *entire* group. It is not your responsibility to ensure that the group's project is as good as it can be, because you don't have enough influence in the large group to do that. Rather, your responsibility is to do your part in the project. It is much the same with your responsibility to vote.

Still, perhaps you're not convinced. Perhaps you think that given the almost-zero chance that your one vote will make the difference in an election, you can't possibly have an obligation to vote. If so, then I ask you to consider this: Maybe whether you have a moral obligation to vote is a little bit tricky—it's a tough question. Ok, but consider the potential moral and personal costs and benefits of voting versus not voting. If you vote, you certainly haven't done anything wrong, and any inconvenience to you is very minimal (assuming you live in an electoral district with decent poll access). If, on the other hand, you don't vote, you have saved yourself a little bit of effort, but you might be doing something pretty seriously immoral.

	possible benefits	possible costs
you vote	• You guarantee that you're doing nothing wrong. • The process of voting is kind of interesting.	• You take a few minutes out of your day.
you do not vote	• You save a few minutes to do something *really* important, like watch another TikTok video.	• You are a first-class, immoral jerk.

Pretty clearly, the morally safe course of action is to vote.

Here's one concern, though. Maybe you don't think the democratic system in your country or state or whatever is very good. Maybe you don't even think very highly of democracy itself. If so, you're in good company. No less a thinker than Plato thought democracy to be a pretty bad form of government. The thing is, we humans have not been able to do any better, at least when it comes to large-scale governance. Democracy enjoys the Winston Churchill defense: "Many forms of government have been tried, and will be tried in this world of sin and woe. No one pretends that democracy is perfect or all-wise. Indeed, it has been said that democracy is the worst form of government except for all those other forms that have been tried from time to time." If you agree that democracy is the worst, except for all the other options, then you must vote.

II. In the Marketplace

Is it ok to ...

6. Is it ok to line up with 16 items in the 15-items-or-fewer lane?

Clarification

Clearly enough, the particular number of items allowed is of no relevance. The same question could be asked about someone queuing in a 10-items-or-fewer lane with 11 items. Let us assume that we are not talking about a situation in which a store is nearly empty and no people are waiting in line to check out. Suppose the store is busy, with fairly long lines for both the "standard" checkouts and the "express" checkout. Further suppose that there is no emergency that requires the shopper to buy urgently needed items quickly.

Con

It is definitely not permissible to try to purchase even one more item than the maximum allowed in the express checkout lane. There are two main arguments that suggest this behavior is immoral. The first involves reasons that are more obviously about what is "moral." The second relies on practical considerations, but because these considerations have to do with the effectiveness of rules in general, it too is an argument about what is moral, or in this case, what is immoral.

The first argument begins with the idea that you are not allowed to make an exception of yourself. Think of the Golden Rule, which can be found in one form or another in the ethical teachings of most religions: Treat others as you would have them treat you. The reason that this ethical rule is found in so many of the world's religions is that it makes a lot of sense. And the reason it makes a lot of sense is that people who violate the Golden Rule are treating themselves as if they were more important than their fellow humans. But, of course, they are not more important than their fellow humans. The person who thinks they're more important than others when they aren't is a … jerk. So, you ought always to obey the Golden Rule.

The second move in the argument is based on an assumption, namely that if people are standing in line for the express lane, you would rather they not line up with more items than they are allowed. So, if the Golden Rule or some variant of it is even roughly correct, then when you line up with more items than you are allowed, you act like a jerk. And acting like a jerk is wrong. Therefore, lining up with more items than you're allowed is wrong.

The second argument calls our attention to a very important fact about rules—that in order for us to make use of a system of rules, we must make those rules precise and rigid. First, rules must be precise in order for them to be followable and enforceable. Imagine a sign in the grocery store that reads "Express Lane—Only a Small Number of Items Allowed." The problem with such a rule is obvious: There is no way to determine what a "small number of items" is. So if the rule is not precise, I really have no way of knowing whether I am allowed to line up with, say, 35 items. The rule, because it is not precise, is not followable. It's also not enforceable. Consider the jackass who lines up in the express lane with two carts overflowing with groceries. Without a precise rule—a rule that specifies the maximum number of items—it's hard to see how we could enforce the rule or justifiably say that the jackass is breaking the rule.

So rules have to be precise in order for them to do any good. But they also have to be rigid. That is, they must not be interpreted so that they allow for minor violations. Here's why: Suppose the sign says "15 items or fewer" and we allow people to line up with 16 items. Lining up with one more item than you're allowed is a minor violation of the rule. If we allowed for this minor violation, then it seems we would be following this principle: If n number of items are allowed, then so are n+1 items. But then, since we just allowed people to line up with 16 items, we have to allow them to line up with 17 items. And then, by our principle, 18 items is also acceptable. And 19 items, and 20, and 21. There is no end to this. By our principle, we are forced to allow people to line up with 1001 items in the express lane. Clearly allowing *that* would defeat the whole purpose of having an express lane in the first place. We got into this ridiculous situation by allowing people to "bend" the rule. But that's just the point—rules shouldn't be bendable.

Their unbendability—their rigidity—is what makes them *rules* in the first place. I conclude that the express lane rule has to be rigid.

In order for the express lane rule to be followable and enforceable, it has to be precise. That means we (or the store, or whoever) have to specify a maximum number of items allowed. In order for the express lane rule to have any point at all—in order for it to accomplish what we want it to accomplish—it must be rigid as well. So, once we decide on the number of items allowed, we should not permit even minor violations of the rule. Anyone who attempts to break the precise and rigid rule undermines the whole point of having the rule in the first place, and hence acts immorally. So, no, you may not line up with even one more item than the express lane allows.

Pro

I can't stand rule fascists. Rule fascists are people who never allow for any exceptions to the rules just because they are the rules. People who say you act immorally by lining up with 16 items in a 15-items-or-fewer express lane are rule fascists. Rule fascism is wrong, and hence it is not morally wrong to act in a way that the rule fascist would object to. Therefore, it is not morally wrong to line up with 16 items in the 15-items-or-fewer lane.

The reason that rule fascism is wrong is that none of us would want to live in a world where exceptions to the rules are not allowed. There are all sorts of reasons why we should allow for occasional or minor violations of rules. The rule fascist is someone who does not trust their fellow humans to use their good judgment and decide when infrequent and minor violations of the rules are permissible. Not only do you not want to live in a world where no exceptions to the rules are *ever* allowed, but you also don't want to live in a world run by rule fascists.

Consider another example. Suppose I have to take a long trip on an airplane and have been forced to take my dog Mortimer with me. Mortimer is a very old basset hound, who I love dearly. Poor ol' Mortimer is put into a carrier and then placed in the special area of the cargo hold of the plane reserved for live animals. After the 12-hour flight, I immediately go to baggage claim to collect Mortimer. He's in his carrier and is clearly not happy. He's whining and whimpering, obviously traumatized by the trip. Mortimer is not in the best health. He needs to take his medicine. He's hungry. He thinks he's been abandoned. I am desperate to get him out of his carrier and comfort him. But the airport has a rule—a very sensible rule—which says that non-human animals must always be inside approved carriers. But wouldn't it be morally ok for me to take Mortimer out of his carrier for just a few minutes? He's a very well-behaved dog, and I know he won't make a mess or cause any trouble for anyone. It is going to take me some time to collect my baggage, go through customs, hail a cab, etc. I'm inclined to say that I would be immoral if I *didn't* take Mortimer out of his carrier right there in the airport. But the rule fascist says that since there is a rule I would be violating if I did so, then it would be wrong for me to comfort my poor, beloved dog. Isn't that enough to show that rule fascism is wrong?

If rule fascism is wrong in the case of Mortimer, then it is also wrong in the case of the express checkout lane. As thinking, sensible people, we can determine when a minor violation of the rules is acceptable. And checking out with 16 items (not 30, not 40) in the 15-items-or-fewer lane is a pretty clear example where a minor violation of the rules is acceptable. Do I really have to forego one of the things I want to buy or join a much, much longer queue? If you say yes, then it seems you're also forced to say that I may not take Mortimer out of his carrier in the airport. But that seems ridiculous.

Think of it this way: The Golden Rule is a good moral rule of thumb. You should try to behave in a way that you would want others to behave in similar circumstances. Note that if you would not be bothered by someone in front of you at the express checkout with 16 items, then you are not violating the Golden Rule by lining up with 16 items yourself. You would not be violating a good, sensible moral rule. You would be violating only a somewhat arbitrary grocery store rule and not causing anyone any real inconvenience in the process.

It is good that we live in a society of rules. Rules about pets roaming free in airports and rules about express checkout lanes make things run more smoothly and allow for society to function in a way that is beneficial to us all. But it is important that we not become slaves to the rules. It is important that we always keep in mind what benefit this or that rule is meant to achieve. And if violating a particular rule does not keep the benefit associated with it from being achieved, then violating the rule is permissible. In the case of the express checkout lane, the benefit associated with the 15-items-or-fewer rule is that shoppers with a few items do not have to waste a lot of time standing in long queues. Since you do not prevent that benefit from being achieved when you line up with 16 items, it is morally permissible for you to do so. Only the rule fascist would object, and we have already seen the problem with rule fascism. (Just think of Mortimer, looking at you with his sad, basset hound eyes through his cage.)

7. Is it ok to not tip at a restaurant?

Clarification

Suppose you go to a restaurant with table service. You get the bill. Is it morally permissible to pay only the amount indicated on the bill and not leave a gratuity? We can ask the question whether the service is exceptional, average, or very bad. Maybe different levels of service correlate with different levels of moral obligation. (There is another, closely related question about what to do when you are given the "opportunity" to tip when you're merely picking up a takeout order or using a rideshare service. There have even been reports of people being asked for tips at self-checkout kiosks! But let us restrict our question so that it is specific to tipping at a sit-down restaurant.)

Pro

I will give two arguments. The conclusion of the first is that it is *sometimes* morally permissible not to tip. The conclusion of the second is that it is *always* morally permissible not to tip.

First, the whole point of tipping is to reward servers who do a particularly good job and to encourage servers to do a good job. When a server gets your order wrong, doesn't check up on you, doesn't refill your water glass, brings your party's food out at different times, etc., they shouldn't be rewarded; they haven't *earned* a tip. Rewarded for what? For doing a poor job? How have they earned anything in addition to their wage just by showing up to work? The whole point of a tip is to reward and to give servers what they have earned, so if you get bad service, you are under no obligation to tip. Sometimes you get bad service at restaurants. Therefore, sometimes it is morally permissible not to tip.

Furthermore, a good case can be made that you *never* have to tip. The reason is that when you tip, you take part in a practice that isn't a good practice, and you can't be obligated to take part in or encourage a bad practice. Tipping at restaurants is a bad practice for a few reasons. First, it defies all explanation that in North America we are expected to tip restaurant servers but not plumbers, grocery store clerks, or doctors. Why do we tip some service providers but not others? I'm pretty sure nobody has a good answer.

The idea that you should tip a percentage of the bill makes no sense either. Suppose you go to one of your favorite restaurants, order the steak and lobster, as well as a glass of Rioja, vintage 1959. Your bill is $200. In most parts of North America, you would be expected to leave $30 or $40 in gratuity. Now suppose that you return to the same restaurant, but this time get the fish and chips and a bottle of beer. Your bill is $30. Now you're expected to tip around $5. Note, however, that the difference in the amount of work done by the server is zero. How on earth does it make any sense for the server to get an extra $35 in the steak-and-lobster scenario, when nothing they have done is any more difficult or time consuming than in the fish-and-chips scenario?

Finally, although we are expected to tip servers in restaurants, we are not expected to tip cooks or dishwashers or bussers. This means that tipping in restaurants encourages a terribly unequal and unfair wage system.

The tipping custom in North America is silly. Much better is the way service wages are dealt with in places such as Japan, where tipping is unheard of (and might be considered rude). There are much better alternatives to the tipping practice. Again, you can't be morally required to partake in a silly practice, and so you are never morally required to tip.

Con

I fear that those who "argue" that you're not morally obligated to tip are really just trying to rationalize their stinginess. Being cheap is one thing. It's quite another to try to convince others that you are *morally praiseworthy* because you're cheap.

Of course you must tip in any situation where it is expected. When you walk into a restaurant with table service, you commit yourself to certain things. You commit yourself to not taking your clothes off halfway through the meal. You commit yourself to being courteous to employees and other patrons. You agree, just by sitting down at a table, that you won't eat food that you purchased from the place next door. You agree that you will pay your bill, and—yes—you agree to leave a tip. Leaving a tip, along with not getting naked, are clauses in an unwritten and unspoken agreement that you sign on to when you decide to eat at a restaurant. For this reason, not tipping is very much like not paying your bill.

Note that as far as your *moral* obligations go, it doesn't matter one bit that it is illegal to dine and dash but legal not to leave a tip. There are many things that are legal but that you shouldn't do. The primary reason why you shouldn't eat and then leave without paying doesn't have anything to do with the illegality of doing so. The main reason why you shouldn't skip out on the bill is that the restaurant has, in effect, promised to serve you food and drink and you have promised to pay for the food and drink in return. Unless you have a very good, unselfish reason for breaking a promise, it is immoral to break it. This is why it is immoral not to pay your bill, and it is also why it is immoral not to leave a gratuity.

It is very clear to all involved that a gratuity is expected. In fact, the expectation is precisely what those who are opposed to tipping object to. Furthermore, the expectation is so widely recognized that in many parts of North America, servers are not paid even the minimum wage because it is assumed that they will take home at least the equivalent of the minimum wage by supplementing their wages with the money they make from tips. In other areas, servers might be paid the minimum wage, but they are paid less than they would be if there were no tipping.

The expectation that you will tip means you have two options: dine at restaurants with table service *and* tip a reasonable amount, or avoid such restaurants in the first place. No restaurateur expects you to eat at their restaurant and you have no moral obligation to do so. You don't have the *right* to dine at a restaurant either, and you certainly don't have the right to dine at a restaurant and not leave a tip. So, if you have a big problem with tipping, your only moral course of action is not to eat out.

8. Is it ok to complain to front-line workers?

Clarification

Front-line workers are the people you actually interact with at a retail store, a government office, a university department, etc. For example, clerks at grocery stores are front-line workers because they are the employees of the grocery store who interact with the store's customers. The question is whether it is morally permissible to complain to these people when there is a problem. For example, suppose you are at a grocery store, trying to purchase a few items, or at the department of motor vehicles, trying to renew your driver's license. It is crowded. There are many lanes or windows, but only two of them are open. You wait and wait. You are frustrated. When you finally make it to the front of the queue, is it morally permissible for you to complain to the front-line worker about the fact that only two of the lanes/windows are open, when all of them should be? Or, to take another example, suppose you get caught in a bureaucratic catch-22, in which the bureaucracy dictates that you must do x before you can do y, but you must do y before you can do x. This kind of situation might involve very important things, such as your university degree, your taxes, your bank accounts, etc. There is obviously a huge problem with the way the bureaucracy is structured and the problem might cause you great consternation. Is it morally permissible for you to complain to a secretary, for example, about the catch-22?

Con

It is not morally permissible to complain to front-line workers for the very simple reason that they are almost never responsible for the problem you have encountered and they almost never have the power to fix the problem. What this means is that when you complain to front-line workers, you make their day worse for no good reason. It is not pleasant to be the recipient of a complaint. Complaints, by their very nature, are not usually delivered in a kind or pleasant way. Complainers are angry. That's why they complain. So, when you complain, the recipient of your complaint is worse off than they would be if you didn't. Now, if your complaint is directed at the person who is responsible for the problem, then the fact that your complaint makes them feel bad is trumped by their responsibility to do their job correctly; in *that* case, it is ok for you to complain. But again, front-line workers are almost never responsible for the cause of your complaint. It is not the grocery store clerk's fault that not enough lanes are open. In fact, if it were within their power to open more lanes, they probably would. But it is not within their power to open more lanes. It is not the department secretary's fault when you encounter a catch-22 at your university, and they can't change the faulty policy. What follows is that when you complain to a front-line worker, your complaint can't possibly change anything. The reason it is immoral to complain is that (a) your complaint can't do any good (because it doesn't do anything to fix the problem) and (b) it does do bad (because it negatively affects the recipient of your complaint).

Pro

Of course it is ok to complain to front-line workers. Part of the reason why we encounter needlessly long lines, bureaucratic catch-22s, and stupid and harmful policies is that not enough people complain. Too many people act like sheep; they are treated badly and they just take it. You shouldn't just take it. You should complain because complaining will have *some* positive effect. Moreover, the more people who complain, the more likely it is that the problem will be fixed. When you don't complain, you are leaving it to others to do what needs to be done. *That* is immoral. Complaining to front-line workers is not only *permissible* but morally *obligatory*.

It is true that it would be better to complain to those who are responsible for the problem and who are in a better position to fix it. But first, it's not as if complaining to front-line workers has *no* effect. If enough complaints are made to front-line workers, those complaints will make their way to the people who have real power. Since people generally don't like being the recipients of complaints, there is a good chance that workers will make the same complaints to their supervisors that people have made to them, so as to save themselves from future unpleasant encounters with the public. Second, it is often not even possible to complain directly to the people who are ultimately responsible for the problem. For example, if a student at my huge, overly bureaucratic university were to get caught in a catch-22, it's not even clear who they could direct their complaint to other than front-line workers, since it is very difficult for a student to even *know* what office or people are responsible for the bad policy. The student's only options would be to either complain to front-line workers or not complain at all. The first option might have a positive effect. The second option will have no effect. Hence, they should complain.

Of course, they should try not to be nasty or abusive. A complaint can be made nicely. Those front-line workers probably have enough problems with their superiors in an institution that produces problems like these.

Option 3—Individuals face a problem with no morally good resolution.

The con essay is correct about the moral problems associated with taking out your frustrations on front-line workers. The pro essay is correct about the moral problems associated with not complaining at all and the difficulty associated with complaining to the right people. What this suggests is that there is no good way of resolving this issue. The real issue is a "big ethics" issue, concerning the proper functions of government bureaucracies and for-profit institutions, as well as the general way in which large societies should be structured. We can try to tackle this big ethics issue, but we can't do anything, as individuals acting alone, about the problems mentioned above. In short, there is no good answer to the question of whether it is ok for you to complain to front-line workers.

9. Is it ok to share access to streaming services?

Clarification

It is common for people to share their usernames and passwords for streaming sites (Netflix, Disney+, Spotify, etc.) with friends and family who are not part of their household. Most streaming services have policies forbidding this practice, and, importantly, it is illegal (or at least legally suspect) in most jurisdictions. But people do it anyway. Our question is whether it is ethical.

Pro

It is not *always* immoral to illegally share access to streaming services. Here is the main argument.

(1) Sharing access is immoral only if it is stealing.
(2) Many cases of sharing access are not stealing.

(3) Many cases of sharing access are not immoral.

The idea behind premise (1) is just that anyone who thinks sharing access is immoral is likely to think so because they think sharing access is a form of theft. The idea is that those who receive the usernames and passwords are depriving streaming services of income.

What about premise (2)? It can be shown to be true by making use of a counterfactual. A counterfactual is a conditional (an if-then statement) where the antecedent (the "if" part) runs counter to fact—i.e., is not true. So, for example, here is a counterfactual: If the sun had blown up yesterday, we wouldn't be here today. This is a counterfactual because the "if" part about the sun blowing up yesterday is false. But note that the entire counterfactual is obviously true. Now, consider this counterfactual, which I will creatively name "counterfactual":

[counterfactual]: If the person who receives the streaming username and password were not able to get the media content via illegal access sharing, then they would not pay the legal market price for the streaming service.

(1) If [counterfactual] is often true, then many cases of sharing access are not stealing.
(2) [counterfactual] is often true.

---

(3) Many cases of sharing access are not stealing.

Now consider a partial definition of stealing and an argument in support of premise (1) in the previous argument.

[necessary condition of stealing]: depriving someone of money, property, credit for their work, or something else of value.

(1) If [counterfactual] is often true, then many cases of sharing access do not satisfy [necessary condition of stealing].
(2) If many cases of sharing access do not satisfy [necessary condition of stealing], then many cases of sharing access are not stealing.

---

(3) If [counterfactual] is often true, then many cases of sharing access are not stealing.

Con

It is always immoral to illegally share access to streaming services. Here is the main argument.

(1) If sharing access is illegal or forbidden because of a reasonable law or policy, then sharing access is immoral.
(2) Sharing access is illegal or forbidden because of a reasonable law or policy.

---

(3) Sharing access is immoral.

The rationale behind premise (1) is that if a law or policy is reasonable, just, and fair, then you must follow it. You are not morally obligated to follow a stupid, unjust, or immoral law or policy; however, you are not allowed to just decide, all on your own, which laws you will follow and which laws you will ignore. You don't get to do that; you're not that important. Consider this argument:

(1) If illegal access sharing is illegal because of a reasonable law, then those who share access treat themselves as more important than the law.

(2) If those who share access treat themselves as more important than the law, then illegal access sharing is immoral.

---

(3) If illegal access sharing is illegal because of a reasonable law, then illegal access sharing is immoral.

What about the reasonability of the law or policy that forbids access sharing? If, as the pro essay claims, access sharing does not always constitute stealing, then what makes the relevant laws and policies reasonable? The answer is that although cases of access sharing aren't *always* cases of stealing, they often are. The purpose of the laws and policies is to prohibit the cases that constitute stealing, and there is no way to prohibit those cases without also prohibiting the cases that don't constitute stealing as well. Since laws and policies must be enforceable, and since there is usually no way for law or policy enforcers to know whether [counterfactual] is true or false, the only way to have an enforceable law or policy that prohibits the access sharing that constitutes stealing is to prohibit all access sharing. Here is the argument in support of the second premise of the main argument.

(1) Illegal access sharing is illegal because of a law that is (a) enforceable and (b) intended to prohibit access sharing that constitutes stealing.

(2) If (1) and if there is no other possible law that has characteristics (a) and (b), then access sharing is illegal because of a reasonable law.

(3) There is no other possible law that has characteristics (a) and (b).

---

(4) Access sharing is illegal because of a reasonable law.

10. Is it ok to save seats in a crowded place?

Clarification

The question has to do with the permissibility of saving seats in any situation where seats are not assigned and where most of the seats are likely to be taken eventually. We might even extend the scope of the question to cover the permissibility of saving places in a queue. Let's assume that the seats you might save are not for people who have already taken their seats and leave to visit the restroom or concession stand or whatever. Let's also assume that if you were to save seats it would be for between two and five additional people. (The question is not asking whether it is ok to save three full rows' worth of seats.)

Pro

If you are inclined to think that it is not ok to save seats for your friends, it's probably because you have a mistaken view of how society functions. Of course I don't mean that you're clueless about how to live in society. Rather, what I mean is that you are making a false assumption about what the basic *units* of society are. More specifically, the primary actors in a cooperative society are often not individuals but rather groups of people. For example, there is no one individual who is *the taxpayers*, and yet any well-functioning society with taxation must take into account the interests of this large group. Any well-functioning society *must* take into account the interests of groups and no society can function well unless groups act in certain ways. Hospitals, universities, municipal governments, charities, and a host of other groups act *as groups* to influence society in a variety of ways.

Note too that the influence and importance of groups is not obviously reducible to the influence or importance of individuals. Here the term "reducible" has a rather technical meaning. If one thing is reducible to another, then a full explanation of the activity of the first can be given in terms of the second alone. To take an example from the philosophy of science, if biology is reducible to organic chemistry, that means that we could, in principle, give a full explanation of all biological stuff using only the language of organic chemistry and referring only to the entities that organic chemistry deals with. If the function of a gene (a biological entity) can be explained fully without referring to genes but only to various protein structures and other molecules (chemical entities), then the function of the gene is thereby reduced. For present purposes, the point is just that it is very questionable whether reduction is always possible. This is true in the physical sciences, such as biology and chemistry, and reduction seems to be even more difficult in the social sciences, such as sociology and political science. It is very difficult to see how we could possibly reduce the actions of the government of the state of New York to the actions of the many individuals who work for the state of New York. In other words, the actions of this group of people are not reducible to the actions of the individuals who make up the group.

But what does all of this have to do with saving seats?! Well, if groups are the primary actors in society, and if group action cannot be reduced to individual action, then we need to acknowledge this fact. In the case of saving seats, we need to acknowledge that there is a group of friends acting as a cohesive unit. It isn't just three or four individuals who go to the movie theater; it is a single *group* that does. Furthermore, for all sorts of reasons it might be the case that the group can only partake in the activity in question if seat-saving is allowed. It is difficult to coordinate a group and the individuals in the group have various commitments. If you are a member of a group going to see a movie (or a play or whatever) and you have to stay late at work so that you have just enough time to get to the theater (or auditorium or whatever) on time, then seat-saving might be the only way that you can join the group. Your friend, who does not have the same kind of work obligations you do, may save a seat for you. If it were immoral for your friend to save the seat for you, then it would be immoral for your group to see the movie (or the play or whatever). But that's ridiculous. If the major actors in society are not just individuals acting alone but also groups, then why would we disallow groups to partake in various activities? There might be some actions that ought to be reserved for individuals, but going to the movies, for example, is clearly not one of them. For the purposes of enforcing traffic laws, it's probably a good idea to designate a single individual—the driver of a car—as the sole individual responsible for the movements of the car. Car driving is something individuals do, and that's as it should be. But for the most part movie-going (or play-going or what have you) is not an individual activity; the vast majority of people who go to the movie theater do so as members of a group, and there is nothing wrong with *that*.

Here's the punchline: If it is true that groups can only partake in a group activity if seats are saved (and in a large number of cases this *is* true), then to say that seat-saving is immoral is pretty much equivalent to saying that it is immoral for groups to partake in such activities. But it clearly *isn't* immoral for groups to partake in such activities. Therefore, saving a few seats for friends is permissible.

Con

An important part of being a moral person is understanding what you are and are not entitled to. For example, you are entitled to listen to music in your home. You are not entitled to listen to it at such a volume that it will disturb your neighbors. It is also important to understand that most entitlements are *conditional*. You are not automatically entitled to drive a car on public streets. You are entitled to drive a car on public streets *on the condition* that you have obtained a driver's license, that your car is in good repair, that you are not inebriated, etc.

Now, just because you are not entitled to something, that doesn't mean that it is immoral to do it. It sounds more than a little weird to say that you're *entitled* to have a dessert both before and after your meal. But as long as you're not doing anything that would bother others by eating two desserts, it is permissible for you to do so. It also seems true that you can be entitled to do something and hence have the moral right to do it, even if doing it *would* bother other people. In a famous US Supreme Court Case, *Cohen v. California*, the court held that Paul Cohen was entitled to enter a courthouse wearing a jacket with the words "Fuck the draft" on it. Now, although the US Supreme Court decides legal cases, not moral issues, you might think that Cohen had a moral entitlement to wear pretty much whatever he wanted into a public building, even though wearing a jacket with

"Fuck the draft" written on it at the height of the Vietnam War was sure to make many people very angry.

What all of this suggests is this: An act is immoral if (a) you are not entitled to do it and (b) doing it would bother other people. (The word "bother" here is intentionally left ambiguous. Should it mean "harm" or "inconvenience" or "offend" or what? That is a difficult question. For now, though, "bother" should serve well enough.)

We are now in a position to see why it is wrong to save seats for your friends at a crowded event. You are entitled to a seat *on the condition* that you have purchased a ticket and on the condition that this particular seat is the one you actually sit down in. You are not entitled to seats for which you have not paid or seats that you do not actually sit down in. Your friends are not entitled to them either. The condition that entitles you or your friends to the extra seats has not been satisfied. So you are not entitled to save the seats. This means that (a) above is satisfied. What about (b)? Well, pretty obviously, if you save seats and others want them, you are inconveniencing those other people. So, yes, other people are bothered by your seat saving. Both (a) and (b) above are satisfied: You are not entitled to the other seats and saving the seats bothers others. The conclusion is that it is immoral for you to save seats at a crowded event.

Also, why do you need to sit next to your friends in the first place? Are you going to talk to each other during a movie or play? Well *that* is certainly immoral. This is perhaps the best argument against seat saving. Maybe seat saving doesn't cause a *huge* inconvenience to others; perhaps it doesn't or shouldn't bother others *too much*. But the flipside is this: not being able to sit next to your friend during a movie or play shouldn't bother you *at all*.

11. Is it ok to eat meat?

Clarification

Some people are vegetarians for ethical reasons. They think it is morally wrong to eat meat. Our question is whether they're right or whether it is morally permissible to consume the flesh of animals.

Con

The typical argument for the immorality of eating meat is straightforward and strong. Here it is:

(1) It is morally wrong to cause needless suffering.
(2) Eating meat causes needless suffering.

---

(3) It is morally wrong to eat meat.

The "needless suffering" referred to here is, obviously enough, the suffering that livestock or hunted animals endure. It is needless because humans do not have to eat meat; maybe a lot of humans *like* to eat meat, but the pleasure they get from eating meat is surely outweighed by the suffering of the animals they eat, especially in factory farming. So the second premise is true.

The first premise is pretty obviously true. It is wrong to make other beings feel pain. There is no reason to think that the physical pain felt by factory-farmed pigs is less morally important than the physical pain felt by humans. Pain is just bad in and of itself, no matter what kind of being is experiencing it.

Since both premises are true and since the argument is valid, the conclusion is true. Hence the argument pretty much seals the deal: You should not eat meat. At the very least, you should be a vegetarian, and if consuming any animal products causes needless suffering, then you should also be a vegan.

There are a few common replies to this argument that fail miserably. One is to claim that humans do in fact need to consume meat to be healthy. This claim is demonstrably false. There is no scientific evidence supporting it and lots of scientific evidence that it's wrong. It is relatively easy to do the research, so if you need convincing, go do it. For now, just note that the American cyclist David Zabriskie raced in the Tour de France on a *vegan* diet in 2011. Riders typically consume about 8,000 calories a day during a race such as the Tour de France. If a top athlete can perform at the top level on a vegan diet, the claim that humans need meat to maintain a healthy body is outrageous.

Another response is that it is "natural" for humans to eat meat. But what does the word "natural" mean here? If it is going to serve as a response to the argument above, the meaning of "natural" is going to have to do a lot of work. Maybe "natural" means that meat-eating was selected for in our evolutionary history. (In the animal world, meat-eaters have their eyes in front; this provides the depth-perception necessary for hunting. Vegetarian animals have their eyes on the sides; this provides vision over a wide angle, so they can look out for predators. Humans have their eyes in front.) But getting from "This is the way humans ate in the ancestral environment" to "It is morally permissible for us to eat that way now" is going to be very difficult. Maybe "natural" means that eating meat "comes naturally," meaning that it is something we do without much effort. But people do lots of bad things without much effort, so it's hard to see how "natural" in this sense is going to serve as a response to the vegetarian's argument. Imagine a tribe of cannibals. For them, killing and eating the members of neighboring tribes comes naturally. It hardly follows that what they do is morally permissible. If the "natural" defense of meat-eating is going to work, you're going to have to find a definition of "natural" that makes it so that (a) it's true that meat-eating is natural for humans and (b) its naturalness is morally relevant. There is no such definition.

A third response I have come across is that if the argument proves that it's wrong for humans to eat cows, chickens, and pigs, then it also shows that it is wrong for lions to eat antelopes, for example. I'm not sure how seriously to take this response, as it seems quite desperate, but it is easy to show why it fails. A lion can't help but eat an antelope, and as far as I can tell, lions are incapable of thinking about morality. For these reasons, morality just doesn't apply in the lion's case. When the lion kills and eats an antelope, what it does is *amoral*—neither morally permissible nor morally impermissible.

Saying that a lion acts immorally when it eats an antelope is a bit like saying that a table acts immorally when you stub your toe on it. Unlike lions, humans are capable of refraining from eating meat and of thinking about morality, so there can be meaningful questions about the morality of *our* diets.

In general, responses to the argument for the ethical obligation to be vegetarian seem to be nothing more than rationalizations, in the worst sense of that term. You are guilty of rationalizing in the bad sense when you first determine what conclusion you want to be true (in this case, that it is ok to eat meat) and *then* go looking for reasons to support it. That's backwards. What you're *supposed* to do as a critical thinker is follow the arguments where they lead. Do the premises in the above argument seem true to you? Yes. Is the argument valid? Yes. So you should accept the conclusion. If you accept the conclusion but continue to eat meat, you thereby act immorally.

Pro

The first thing to notice about the standard vegetarian argument is that it doesn't really show that it is *always* wrong to eat meat. For example, it is hard to see how the argument could show that it would be wrong for you to eat roadkill or an animal that dies of old age. Suppose I unintentionally hit a deer with my car and kill it. No doubt I will have caused the deer lots of suffering, but since I didn't intend to, I can't be faulted for that, assuming that I was driving in a responsible manner. Would I be doing anything morally wrong if I took the deer carcass home, dressed it, cooked the meat, and ate it? It doesn't seem so.

Now of course the important issue isn't about eating roadkill, but the example is instructive. The reason it would be ok for me to eat the deer I accidentally killed is that my *eating* the deer doesn't cause any needless suffering. The damage was already done when I hit the deer. What this shows is that we have to pay close attention to the causal connection between our eating animals and their suffering. The first premise in the vegetarian argument is right. It is wrong to cause needless suffering. What we have to ask, then, is when and how our meat-eating causes suffering, and what causal effects a vegetarian diet might have.

With that in mind, consider three responses to the argument in the con essay. The first is not a full response to the argument. It is half a response to the argument and half a way of recognizing the vegetarian's ethical concerns without going all the way to saying that eating meat is always wrong. You might think, quite reasonably, that factory farming is a needlessly cruel practice. (If you really want to see how factory-farmed chicken is produced [you don't], go to YouTube and search "mercy for animals Tyson.") But what about eating happy livestock? If you live in the developed world, you can make efforts to eat animals that were not factory farmed. So instead of eating tortured chickens, you can try to eat chickens that frolicked about in a farmyard and were humanely killed before they even knew what hit them. It's not clear that any *suffering* is involved when livestock is treated well and then killed for human consumption. What we might say, then, is that although it is morally wrong to eat factory-farmed meat, it is morally permissible to eat well-treated animals.

You might worry about prematurely *ending the life* of livestock, but note two things. First, the argument in the con essay doesn't say anything about *killing* animals. That is not the reason that was given for thinking that it is wrong to eat meat. Second, you might think that it is not morally problematic to end the life of something that has no *interest* in staying alive. Presumably plants do not want to stay alive, and that is part of the reason why we think it is morally permissible to kill and eat them. A chicken, for example, might be much the same. Does a chicken have a conception of self—a conception of I? Does a chicken want to continue living? It's a difficult question, but suffice it to say that it's not unreasonable to think that a chicken doesn't have any interest in staying alive and hence that it is ok to painlessly kill it in order to eat it.

The second response to the vegetarian argument is a denial of the second premise, which says that eating meat causes needless suffering. We have already seen how eating meat might not necessarily cause any suffering at all, but we can also question the "needless" part of the premise. The con essay is right that humans don't have to eat meat to be healthy. But humans do have to eat *something* to remain healthy. If you're not eating animals or animal products, then you're eating plants. But large-scale horticulture causes lots of animal suffering. If you have ever had the experience of seeing a wheat field harvested with a combine, you know that many, many rodents and birds are killed and injured in the process. A lot of animal suffering is involved in harvesting a wheat field. What this suggests is that if it is wrong to eat meat because it causes needless suffering, then it is also wrong to eat bread because it causes needless suffering. But now we're losing the sense in which the suffering involved is really "needless." On the assumption that we humans are allowed to do what it takes to live, and if both animal agriculture and horticulture cause animal suffering, then since we don't have any other options, the suffering caused is not needless. To say that we act immorally no matter what we do is to suggest that it is immoral for us to do what it takes to live. That's preposterous. This suggests that the second premise in the vegetarian argument is false.

The third response to the vegetarian argument is another attack on the second premise. The second premise is arguably ambiguous. On one reading it is this:

A lot of people eating a lot of meat causes needless suffering.

Understood this way, the premise is very plausible. But as a single individual, you don't have a lot of say in whether the suffering occurs or not. There are lots of people eating meat, and it is going to be hard for you to put an end to that phenomenon. So on this first reading, the second premise makes the vegetarianism issue a "big ethics" issue, and not one that you can resolve in your day-to-day life. In order to eliminate the suffering involved, we would need a huge societal change, and the ethics of huge societal changes is not everyday ethics. In order to make the vegetarianism issue relevant to individuals making personal ethical choices, we would need to understand the second premise this way:

You eating meat causes needless suffering.

On this reading, the premise makes the ethics of meat consumption relevant to the choices you make today about what to eat. Fine. The problem now, though, is that the premise thus understood is false. How much suffering are *you* going to prevent by adopting a vegetarian diet? Not much. Factory farming will still go on. The people making money from factory farming will not notice that you left the meat-eating club, because your new diet is not going to affect their bottom line. It is all well and good to celebrate "the power of one," but the fact is that your personal diet choices don't have a lot of power. Hence, even if it were good for everyone or almost everyone to stop eating meat, it doesn't follow that you are morally required to stop eating meat.

III. School and the Workplace

Is it ok to ...

12. Is it ok to cheat in a class?

Clarification

There are many ways that college or university students might cheat. They might use ChatGPT or another large language model without permission, plagiarize in some other way, pay someone to write an essay, copy one of their classmate's answers on a test, etc. The question is simply whether it is ever morally permissible to cheat.

Con

Of course it is wrong to cheat. Cheating is lying for selfish reasons. Although it might be permissible to lie on some occasions, it is never permissible to lie just to benefit yourself.

Furthermore, cheating harms our educational institutions and the value of education generally. It is already the case that a university degree in North America doesn't really count for all that much; it is now about as valuable as a high school degree used to be. There are several reasons why, including grade inflation and the fact that many more people are attending universities than in the past, including people who aren't really interested in becoming better educated. Cheating is another factor. If cheating is widespread, and if students get away with cheating and ultimately "earn" a degree, then students with university degrees are likely to be less capable than if cheating weren't widespread. Eventually employers and others discover that just because someone has a degree, that doesn't mean they are ready to competently do the kinds of things that we used to be able to expect from people who graduated from college or university.

Relatedly, cheating is wrong because the cheater wouldn't want other students to cheat. What if everyone cheated? What would happen to our colleges and universities?

Finally, cheating is morally impermissible because when cheating goes on, it's not fair to those students who don't cheat. It is immoral to be unfair, and hence it is immoral to cheat.

Pro

The reason why I think it is morally permissible to cheat is just that I see no good reason to think otherwise. Consider the arguments made in the con essay. They all fail. The first argument depends on the assumption that it is always wrong to lie to benefit yourself. It is very questionable whether this assumption is true. Sometimes people ask me to social gatherings. Sometimes I don't want to go. On those occasions I just lie and say I already have other plans. I don't lie to spare the feelings of the person who invites me or anything like that. I lie because (a) I don't want to go, and (b) lying is just the easiest way not to go. When I lie in these situations, I lie for my own benefit, but it is very unclear that such lying is morally wrong. At the very least, the person who thinks it is always wrong to lie for your own benefit owes us an argument.

The second argument in the con essay makes the point that university degrees mean a lot less than they used to. This is certainly true, but other factors, including those mentioned in the con essay, play much more of a role in the devaluing of college and university degrees. It is just an implausible stretch to say that cheating is a significant factor.

The third argument asks the question, "What if everyone cheated?" But if you're contemplating cheating, one of the things you *already know* is that not everyone will cheat. Hence it's not clear what point is being made by the "what-if" question.

The fourth argument says that the cheater is being unfair to those who don't cheat. I don't understand. Those who don't try to cheat could if they wanted to. Other students have just as much of an opportunity to cheat as the cheater has. They just choose not to take that opportunity. Saying that the cheater is being unfair to the non-cheaters is a bit like saying that the student who studies hard is being unfair to the students who don't study hard.

Cheating might not be a good idea, primarily because you might get caught. Most instructors will try to catch cheaters and penalize them. It is morally permissible for instructors to do so. Still, those who think that it is *immoral* to cheat need better arguments than those presented in the con essay.

13. Is it ok to use plagiarism-detection software?

Clarification

One version of the question is whether it is ok for instructors to use tools designed to detect writing produced by large language models such as ChatGPT. But since large language models capable of fooling instructors, as well as the methods for detecting their use, are still fairly young as of this writing, we will leave that particular version for another time. For now we will focus on this version: Is it ok for instructors to use software that is designed to detect plagiarism that takes the form of copying from journal articles, websites, previously submitted student papers, etc.

You probably already have an idea of how this kind of software works: Students submit work to be evaluated by their instructor and the software compares their submissions to a huge database of books, articles, internet content, and previously submitted student papers. The software then checks for any matches. Such software is used at thousands of colleges and universities and the service is sold to them by for-profit companies. Our question is whether it is morally permissible for instructors to in effect force their students to have their work inspected by plagiarism-checking software. A related question is whether it would be ok for students to refuse to submit their work to be checked in this way.

One point of confusion about the software should be addressed before we get to the arguments. Some of my students seem to be under the impression that the software judges students to be guilty or not guilty of plagiarism all by itself and that instructors blindly follow what it says. This is not true. The software typically indicates to an instructor what percentage of a student's paper matches other sources. Matches of 2% or 3% are very common and are usually not indicative of cheating. The instructor is able to call up the other sources and do the comparison themself. It is the instructor who decides whether there might be some academic dishonesty going on, not the software, which simply aids the instructor in trying to combat the very prevalent problem of plagiarism.

Pro

It is morally permissible for an instructor to use plagiarism-checking software for the same reason that it is morally permissible for an instructor to do a Google search if they *suspect* plagiarism. Suppose an instructor gets a paper that (a) doesn't quite follow the directions of the assignment, and (b) is very well written. Suppose further that their school does not have a subscription to any plagiarism-checking services. Would it be permissible for the instructor to search for passages from the student's paper on Google? I think the answer is obviously yes. Otherwise, we would be forced to say that it is not morally permissible for instructors to try to catch cheaters, but that's ridiculous.

The only difference between an instructor using Google to catch cheaters and using the software is that the software might be able to catch cases of plagiarism that the instructor plus Google would never catch. For example, students sometimes plagiarize papers submitted previously by students who took the same course a few years ago. It is unlikely that the instructor will have any reason to think that plagiarism has occurred in such a case, and furthermore the past student's paper is unlikely to be anywhere on the internet. If, on the other hand, the past student's paper is in the relevant database, the instance of plagiarism will probably be caught. Again, the software is just a more effective way of doing what an instructor would do anyway if they wanted to guard against cheating.

Another analogy that might be helpful in seeing why the use of plagiarism-checking software is morally permissible involves referees, umpires, and instant replay in professional sports. Nobody thinks it is wrong for referees to be on the field, even though one of their primary functions is to detect cheating. Nobody thinks that players are being treated as "guilty until proven innocent" just because officials are on the field, trying to catch rule breakers. Finally, whatever problems traditionalists might have with instant replay, they don't object to it on the grounds that it is unfair or unjust or anything like that. Now make the analogy: The officials are the instructors, instant replay is the software, the players are the students, and the rules about what constitutes cheating are the rules about what constitutes plagiarism. It's hard to see how there is anything that is both (a) disanalogous and (b) morally relevant in the two analogues. Thus, if you think that refereeing and the use of instant replay in professional sports is morally permissible, then you should also think that the use of the software is morally permissible.

Con

It is true that there is nothing to the "guilty until proven innocent" complaint. There is, however, a closely related complaint that has a lot of merit. It is that the automatic use of plagiarism-checking sets up an unhealthy environment for the student–teacher relationship. It makes the student–teacher relationship less cooperative and more confrontational. Real education does not involve a competition between student and teacher, but rather involves the two working together to achieve a common goal. Imagine the instructor who has video cameras installed in their classroom in order to monitor their students, who visits their students' houses unannounced to check that they really are sick, who grills students about the nature of their learning disabilities, and who generally treats their students with a lot of mistrust. Such an instructor can truthfully say that they are not treating their students as guilty until proven innocent, but they cannot truthfully say that they aren't poisoning the relationship they have with their students. The use of plagiarism-checking software is just a less severe case of poisoning the relationship, and that is why it is morally questionable.

I say only "questionable" because the main reason that instructors use the software in the first place is that plagiarism is rampant. It is the students, not the instructors, who poisoned the student–teacher relationship to begin with. Instructors are just trying to salvage what they can, and to do so they must try to catch cheaters. The software offers a fairly effective tool to help them do that. For this reason, the argument I just gave should only make you *question* the use of the software. I don't think the argument is conclusive.

But let me now present another argument that should seal the deal. This argument doesn't have so much to do with the student–teacher relationship or the educational environment. Rather, it concerns the exploitation of students by corporations. As was mentioned in the clarification section, the software in question is sold to colleges and universities by for-profit companies. Also mentioned was the fact that student papers are added to databases so that they can be compared with future submissions. What this means is that students' work is being used by these companies to make money. Insofar as students have agreed to this arrangement, it is only because they must if they want to take courses at a college or university that subscribes to a plagiarism-checking service. Moreover, students are never offered a cut of the companies' profit. In fact, students actually *pay* for the privilege of having their work used by a for-profit company, since their tuition fees help to pay for their school's subscription. Students who submit papers through the checking software are adding to a company's database, and the software would not be nearly as effective if this weren't so. Hence, when students submit papers, they are helping companies to produce a more attractive product that can be sold for more money. Hence, when instructors force their students to use plagiarism-checking services, they are in effect forcing students to economically exploit themselves. Instructors are forcing students to hand over the fruits of their labor so that someone else can make a buck off of it *and* they are making students pay so that this can happen. That is wrong, and it is the main reason why it is not morally permissible for instructors to subject their students to the software.

Option 3—Things Get Complicated.

Here's the thing: At least at my university, when I set up an assignment, I have the option of making it so that my students' papers will *not* be added to a database. My students' papers are still compared to the existing database, but they are not added to it. By default, the submissions go into the database, but I can turn that off. So now our question might be: Is it ok for instructors to use the software *if* their students' papers are not added to the database? On the one hand, if an instructor makes it so that submissions do not go into the database, then maybe they get around the exploitation concern raised in the con essay. On the other hand, if an instructor changes the default setting, then they are doing something that they couldn't possibly want other instructors to do, since the software is way more effective when past student papers are in the database. If the instructor changes the default setting, they make a moral exception of themself and their students. They are in effect saying that they want *other* students to have their work used to turn a profit (so that the software will work well for the instructor) but they don't want this to happen to *their* students (because of the concern raised in the con essay). Making a moral exception of yourself or the people you're acting on behalf of is morally wrong.

It's starting to look like instructors are damned if they do and damned if they don't. There are roughly three competing moral considerations involved:

(1) Instructors should try to catch cheaters using the most effective means at their disposal.
(2) Instructors should not aid in the exploitation of their students.
(3) Instructors should not make a moral exception of themselves or their students.

It might be impossible for instructors to obey all three imperatives. If they do not use plagiarism-checking software, they violate (1). If they do use the software with the default database setting, they violate (2). If they use the software and change the default database setting, they violate (3). And now they're all out of options. This situation has the makings of a true moral dilemma (actually a *trilemma*). What is a poor instructor to do? What are students to do, knowing that their instructors face this dilemma?

14. Is it ok to complain to an instructor about how a course is taught?

Clarification

The question is not about whether it is permissible for students to seek clarification form their instructors about what is expected in an assignment, why they received the grade they did, or how they might do better on future assignments or tests. All of these are clearly permissible and should even be encouraged. The question is not about whether it is permissible for students to complain about instructors who are simply not doing their jobs—when an instructor doesn't show up for class, or regularly shows up late, or doesn't return graded assignments. Everyone can agree, I think, that when someone is assigned a job, doesn't do it, and their failure negatively affects other people, those people are in the right when they complain. The question *is* about whether it is morally permissible for students to *challenge* their instructors on aspects of courses, for example by claiming that an assigned grade is "subjective" or "arbitrary," or saying that an assignment is "unfair" or "unreasonable," or arguing that different material should be covered in a course, or that the material should be presented in a different way.

Pro

Students are entitled to expect certain things from a course, and if those things aren't present, then of course they have the right to complain. Imagine enrolling in Introduction to Philosophy and on the first day of class the instructor announces that they're tired of teaching philosophy and that instead the course is going to be on differential equations. It would obviously be morally appropriate for students to complain in this scenario. Furthermore, reasonable expectations extend well beyond the general topic to be covered in a course. To take another extreme example, suppose I have lost my keys and I tell my students that for today's class period students will spend the allotted time searching for them—that anyone who makes an honest attempt to find my keys will get a B on the next test, anybody who refuses to look gets an F on the next test, and the student who finds my keys will get an A+ in the course. Clearly, students would be right to complain. Finally, suppose that an instructor tells their students that the way they are going to grade the final essays is by taking the entire stack of printed essays to the top of a flight of stairs and then throwing the stack down the stairs. Any essays that land on the top third of the stairs get Ds, essays that land on the middle third get Cs, essays that land on the bottom third get Bs, and any essays that make it all the way down the stairs to the floor below get As.

These over-the-top cases involve, respectively, the material covered in a course, the assignments in a course, and the grading method. In all of the over-the-top cases, it would certainly be morally permissible for students to complain. In more realistic cases, it is morally permissible for students to complain for the very same reasons that it is morally permissible for them to complain in the over-the-top cases. The only difference between realistic cases and over-the-top cases is a matter of degree. In other words, in the over-the-top cases, the instructors' behavior is *really* bad, and in some actual cases the instructor's behavior is a little less bad. But it can still be bad even if it is not *as* bad. When your instructor acts badly, you are in the moral right if you complain. Surely it is true that some instructors sometimes act badly in their capacity as instructors, and hence it is at least sometimes morally permissible for students to complain.

Con

It is true that it would be morally permissible for students to complain if their instructors were acting badly in their capacity as instructors. However, it is almost never the case that students who think their instructors are acting badly are correct. Usually, students' complaints about material covered, grading method, or assignments have nothing to do with fairness or reasonable expectations. Rather, the complaints are almost always the result of students getting upset when an outcome is not the one they desired.

The fairness issue is an important one. This seems to be a common complaint—that something about a course is "unfair." But the students who make this charge don't seem to understand what "fair" means in the first place. Here's a hint: fairness is not you getting what you want. Fairness involves equal treatment (where "equal" does not mean "same") and the consistent application of transparent standards. Instructors (or departments or universities or whatever) set the standards for their courses and tell their students what those standards are. Surely *that* is not unfair. Hence, as long as instructors apply those standards in a consistent way to everyone, students are not in a good moral position if they choose to complain.

Consider an example of the "unfair" complaint. I sometimes teach an advanced (third-year) philosophy of mind course. The prerequisite for the course is a lower-level philosophy of mind course. One year, a student wrote the following on a course evaluation:

"The readings in this class were mostly very very challenging, especially for a non-philosophy major. Thus, holding high expectations for the response papers, I found, were unfair and unreasonable."

It's hard to know where to begin here. This student took a *third-year* course *in philosophy* which *has a prerequisite*, and they seem to think that I was unfair because I assigned challenging readings and because they are not a philosophy major. Good grief. The student used the word "thus" so it seems they think that some reasons have been given for what follows the "thus". Let's reconstruct the argument.

(1) The readings [in this upper-division philosophy course with a prerequisite] were challenging.
(2) I am not a philosophy major.

---

(3) Brian acted unfairly in holding us to high standards on our papers covering the readings.

I will leave it as an exercise for the reader to indicate why this is a bad argument. For now, it is enough to note that it is a really bad argument. Moreover, it is almost *always* the case that when students say an instructor is "unfair" or "unreasonable" they base their charge on really bad arguments like this. Again, I can only guess that most complaints about unfairness are based on a misunderstanding of what fairness is and what it isn't, but the main point is this: It is just straight-up immoral to accuse someone of a moral failing (e.g., being unfair, being racist, being an ax murderer) when you have no idea what you're talking about. Students almost always have no idea what they're talking about when they complain about how a course is conducted. Therefore, it is almost always wrong for students to complain in this manner.

15. Is it ok to ignore your moral convictions in order to do your job?

Clarification

The classic example in which this question might arise involves a CEO or board of directors for a large, publicly traded company, who has two options concerning the future course of the company. The first option would benefit (or at least not harm) society, but would not significantly increase profits. The second option would increase profits, but might do harm to society. Think of a large manufacturer in the United States that can either keep a large number of union-ized workers employed with a living wage and benefits, or move all of those jobs overseas, where they will be filled by people who will be paid a pittance without any benefits. Arguably, the CEO's job is to increase profits for the benefit of shareholders. But suppose they have a serious moral objection to exporting the jobs. Is it ok for them to do so anyway?

Note that you don't have to be a CEO or even very high-ranking in order for you to feel as if your job requires you to do things that you don't think are morally right. I once worked at a movie theater. It was surrounded by several bars and restaurants. The theater opened at about 10:30 in the morning, even though the first movies didn't screen until about noon. This meant that on weekdays there was a period of time in the late morning during which the theater was the only place open for business in the area. My boss—a less than bril-liant guy named Eddie—strictly enforced a policy stating that use of the restrooms was reserved for patrons of the theater only. More than once it happened that while I was setting up in the morning, someone would come in and ask to use the restroom. At least once, the individual was obviously desperate: he had an emergency bath-room situation. But I always did as my boss instructed and told these unfortunate people that they could not use the restroom. I always felt like a complete ass doing so. The question is whether I acted morally.

Con

By definition of "moral conviction," it is not morally permissible for you to ignore your moral convictions just because your job requires you to do so. (By the way, what does "requires" really mean here? The Earth isn't going to explode if you disobey an immoral policy.) If you have a belief that certain kinds of actions are immoral, but you only refrain from doing those kinds of actions when it is convenient for you, then your belief isn't a moral conviction. It's not even clear that you really believe what you think you believe. For example, it's easy enough not to steal and to have the "conviction" that it is wrong to steal when you don't really have the opportunity to steal anything, or when stealing would require a lot of effort on your part. Your supposed moral conviction isn't doing anything in a case where you aren't tempted to steal anyway. The only time a moral conviction serves any useful purpose is when you're tempted to do something that would be immoral. If you are tempted to steal something, but your deeply-held moral beliefs prevent you from stealing, then your deeply-held moral beliefs have done their job. If, on the other hand, you are tempted to steal something and suddenly you don't seem to have any deeply-held moral beliefs about stealing anymore, then it's hard to see how you have any moral convictions at all. It is very easy to just *say* or *think* that a certain kind of action is wrong, but merely saying and thinking don't count for much, morally speaking. What really counts is what you actually *do*. You can't really tell whether you yourself have a moral conviction until the going gets tough. If, when the going gets tough, you don't act in accordance with your supposed convictions, then you act immorally. Hence, if the requirements of your job are enough for you to ignore what you think is right and wrong, then when you fulfill those requirements you act immorally. It's tempting to say that you aren't even a moral person.

If you *really* believe that it is wrong to do x, if you're *convinced* that it is wrong to do x, then what could explain you doing x just because you think you have to in order to do your job? The answer is a phenomenon called weakness of the will. You experience weakness of the will when you realize what the best course of action is, but due to strong desires, cowardice, addiction, or whatever, you do not take that course of action. We all experience weakness of the will from time to time, and not just in morally salient situations. Laziness and procrastination are good examples of weakness of the will. I know I really should do my grading now on Friday. It will make my weekend much more enjoyable. But I'm lazy. I think, "Why put off until tomorrow what you can put off until the day after tomorrow?" even though I *know* the policy I'm following is a stupid one that is not in my best interest. So instead of grading I waste an incredible amount of time watching YouTube videos. I am later forced to ruin part of my weekend with grading.

In the grading case, my weak will may or may not be an example of an ethical failing on my part. It depends on what the correct view is on ethical duties to oneself. But in the case where my weak will caused me to turn away people who were desperate to use a restroom, it was certainly an ethical failing on my part. I acted immorally because I simply didn't have the moral courage to run the small risk of receiving a mild reprimand from my boss in order to do what I thought was right. Now, in my case, both the penalty I would have received had I done the morally right thing and the wrongness of what I actually did were minimal. That doesn't change the fact that what I did was wrong. Note too that it is often the case that as the potential penalty goes up (from mild reprimand to demotion to being fired) so does the potential wrongness (from refusing someone with a full bladder to causing mild environmental damage to ruining the lives of many people). In cases where the wrongness of doing x is huge and the penalty for not doing x is small, it might be easy to do the right thing. But such cases are few and far between. It is not easy being moral, and weakness of the will is by its very nature an incredibly difficult thing to fight. Still, you must fight it in order to act morally. The upshot is that you must do what you think is right even if doing what you think is right means that you lose your job.

Pro

There are three reasons why it might be morally permissible to put your moral convictions aside for the sake of doing your job.

(1) If it were not ok for people to put their moral convictions aside in order to do their jobs, then a lot of people—maybe *most* people—wouldn't be able to do their jobs at all. To take an extreme example, consider the Marxist. There are more than a few Marxists who live in capitalist societies. As Marxists, they think that capitalism is an unjust system, and they think that it is immoral to do anything that fosters capitalism. But if they take *any* job, it will be a job within a capitalist system, regardless of whether they work for a for-profit entity or a charity or a think tank. No matter what you think about Marxism or the moral convictions of Marxists, it is more than a little weird to say that Marxists living in capitalist societies shouldn't take any job at all. But the person who says that it is not morally permissible to set aside your moral convictions in order to do your job seems to be committed to saying just that—if you think capitalism is wrong, you're only moral option is to be unemployed. This result serves as a refutation of the con side all by itself.

(2) If you don't put your moral convictions aside to do your job, you will simply be replaced by someone who doesn't have any moral qualms about doing what you take to be immoral. That result is actually *worse* than you doing what you can from the inside to change things for the better while in the meantime doing what you take to be immoral. For example, I am very sympathetic to the view that the entire system of grading used at most universities is misguided and that it borders on being immoral. There are a variety of reasons for thinking that assigning letter grades to students is not pedagogically sound. In other words, there is reason to think that the way we use grades in universities is detrimental to education. It's not much of a stretch to conclude that the common grading system is immoral. Now, here I am, an instructor at a university. What am I to do? Well, if I refuse to assign grades on moral grounds, I will probably lose my job. Assuming I am replaced by someone else who doesn't really care about whether the common grading system is good or bad, how has anything improved? The person who replaces me might not be as good a teacher as me and they aren't going to do anything to fix what I take to be a problem. It would be better if I advocated for a change to the way we evaluate students at my university, even if doing so requires that in the interim I assign the stupid letter grades at the end of every term.

(3) Relatedly, there is a moral cost associated with *not* doing your job as you are expected to do it. For one, in taking a job you agree to do certain things. Even if you find some of those things objectionable, you are in effect breaking a promise if you don't do them. Second, many people with jobs have moral obligations to dependents. If I just up and quit my job for moral reasons, what is going to happen to my daughter? I have a moral obligation to feed, shelter, and clothe her. It's unlikely that I will be able to find any job that doesn't require me to do *something* that I find morally objectionable (see point (1)). Yet I still have to take care of my daughter; my moral obligations to her are probably going to outweigh my moral obligation not to do things in my job that I think are objectionable.

Option 3—It depends.

Obviously enough, the defense that goes "I was just doing my job" doesn't always work. The commonly used and extreme example of the ridiculousness of this defense is when it was used by people whose job it was to help exterminate people in the Nazi concentration camps. Equally obvious is that sometimes other considerations rightly trump your moral convictions about doing your job. The pro essay provides examples. What would be really nice—and what we don't have—is an easy way of determining when these other considerations really do trump your moral convictions about doing your job and when they don't. There are easy cases at the extremes: The soldier at the concentration camp should do everything in his power not to do his job well. The single parent supporting six children by herself shouldn't quit her job because it requires her to enforce restroom policies she thinks are unreasonable. Again, these are easy cases, but the reason it is difficult to be moral is that there are a lot of difficult cases too. How should a well-meaning person adjudicate these difficult cases? Maybe we are forced to say that they just have to do their best; they have to guard against weakness of the will, they have to try to put aside selfish motivations, they have to try to determine what kind of person they would be if they took this option or that option, and then decide accordingly. Doing all of that is already very hard, but that is what morality requires.

16. Is it ok to go to work or school sick?

Clarification

This question is pretty straightforward. As a university instructor, I have often agonized over it. Often I teach courses that meet just once a week for only twelve weeks, so if I miss just one class period, it's kind of a big deal. For that reason, I have taught classes when I felt like death warmed over. I can function half-way decently when I'm sick, I think, but I always wonder whether I'm doing the right thing.

Con

(1) If you go to work/school sick, then you are likely to make other people sick.
(2) If you are likely to make other people sick, then you make the world a worse place.
(3) You have a moral obligation not to make the world a worse place.

---

(4) You have a moral obligation not to go to work/school sick.

Pro

(1) If you do not go to work/school sick, then you will not do what is expected of you.
(2) If you do not do what is expected of you, then you make the world a worse place.
(3) You have a moral obligation not to make the world a worse place.

---

(4) You have a moral obligation to go to work/school sick.

Option 3—It depends.

(1) If you are sick you must either go to work/school or not go to work/school.

(2) If you go to work/school sick, then you make the world a worse place.

(3) If you do not go to work/school sick, then you make the world a worse place.

---

(4) If you are sick you make the world a worse place (no matter whether you go to work/school sick or not).

(5) If you will make the world a worse place no matter what you do, then you must do a cost–benefit analysis to determine the moral course of action.

---

(6) In order to determine whether it is moral to go to work/ school sick, you must do a cost–benefit analysis.

The cost–benefit analysis will need to consider a variety of factors: how important it is that you be at work or school on the day in question, how sick you are and with what illness, how contagious you are likely to be, whether you are likely to be in *close* contact with others, etc. You probably will not be able to come up with an algorithm, assign numbers, and do the math to determine whether you should go to work or school, but you should be able to do a kind of qualitative cost–benefit analysis in order to come up with a best estimate about what is right to do.

IV. Friends and Family

Is it ok to ...

17. Is it ok to lie to people to spare their feelings?

Clarification

Unless someone is a friend or at least a close acquaintance, you are unlikely to be in a situation where you might lie to them for their own benefit. So let us say that the "people" referred to in the question are your friends. There are two importantly different kinds of circumstances in which you might ask the question. One kind of situation occurs when either you or your friend could easily change whatever it is that is tempting you to lie. For example, imagine your friend is wearing a hat that makes her look ridiculous. She excitedly asks, "What do you think of my new hat?" Should you lie to her? This is an easily changeable situation because if you say anything like, "No, it ... doesn't flatter you," then if she so chooses she can simply remove the hat. To consider an example of the second kind of situation, suppose that your friend gets a new haircut. She has shorn off her beautiful long hair and is now sporting a green-dyed reverse mohawk. It just doesn't work on her. She asks, "What do you think of my hair?" This is a situation that is not easily changeable because your friend can't very well undo her haircut. In the essays below, this distinction is ignored, but it is an important one. You might reasonably think that it is wrong to lie in the easily changeable case but permissible or even obligatory to lie in the not-easily-changeable case. So keep the distinction in mind.

The question is about sparing your friends' *feelings*. We're not asking whether it is ok to lie to friends for their own safety, or anything like that. The potentially bad thing that will happen if you do not lie is that your friends will feel embarrassed or ashamed, sad or angry.

Pro

The answer is obviously "yes." A more challenging question is whether it is morally *obligatory* to lie to people to spare their feelings. I might be inclined to say that even then, the answer is "yes." At any rate, surely it is *permissible*.

You can choose to speak the truth about a particular topic, or lie, or say nothing. Associated with each of these options are three potential outcomes: you make the person you're speaking to feel better, you make them feel worse, or what you say has no effect on their emotional state. So there are nine possibilities: speak the truth and it makes someone feel better, lie and it make someone feel worse, say nothing and your silence makes them feel worse, etc. Luckily, we can focus on just three possibilities:

(A) You say nothing to your friend and that has no effect on their emotional state.

(B) You say nothing to your friend and that makes them feel better.

(C) You lie to your friend and that makes them feel better.

My argument is this: (A) is ok. If (A) is ok, then so is (B). And if (B) is ok, then so is (C). Therefore, it is ok to lie to your friend to make them feel better. Let's look at each premise in the argument:

(A) is ok: This premise is correct because you can't possibly have a moral obligation to always be saying something about every topic imaginable. This is especially obvious if your silence doesn't have any negative effects.

If (A) is ok, then (B) is ok: Isn't this just obvious? If doing something (remaining silent) is ok when it has no effect, then surely doing that same something is ok when it has an overall positive effect.

If (B) is ok, then (C) is ok: Note that if (B) is ok then you don't always have a moral responsibility to speak the truth. Why? Because saying nothing is ... not speaking the truth. If you think your friend's hat looks ridiculous on them but you say nothing, then you are not telling them the truth about how their hat looks. You're not telling the truth because you're not "telling" anything. Again, making someone feel better by not telling the truth is ok. That's what's going on in (B). But it's also what's going on in (C). So, if (B) is ok, then so is (C).

It seems the only way to block the argument is to say there's something especially bad about lying, as opposed to not saying anything. But *that* claim seems highly implausible. Suppose an ax murderer wants to kill my friend Marvin and asks me where Marvin is. If I refuse to tell the ax murderer about Marvin's whereabouts, it seems I've done a good thing, right? But if that's true, then I also do a good thing when I *lie* to the ax murderer about where Marvin is. If anything, lying is *better* than saying nothing in this case (because if I lie to the ax murderer, I might be able to divert him away from Marvin in a way that I couldn't if I merely remained silent). The lesson is this: When the potential consequences are good, it is ok to not speak the truth by remaining silent. What this shows is that when the potential consequences are good, it is also ok to not speak the truth by lying. So, it is certainly ok for you to lie to people to spare their feelings.

Con

I'm sure you have heard the aphorism "Honesty is the best policy." There is much truth in it, but not just because it implies that truth telling is morally good. It says more than that. The aphorism says truth telling is a good *policy*. What is a policy? Often the employees at retail stores will tell customers that they cannot do this or that because it is against "store policy." This can be frustrating for customers, especially if there seems to be good reason to allow for an exception to the policy in a particular instance. But that is the nature of a policy: it's a straight-up rule, not merely a suggestion. Assuming that the store has good reason to follow that policy *as a policy*, that means it has good reason not to allow for exceptions to it. Now, the aphorism above is obviously not about a store's policy. It is about personal policy—your policy. So for present purposes, we can define a policy as a personal rule that you have decided to live by, pretty much no matter what. What "Honesty is the best policy" really means, then, is that you should decide to adopt the policy of telling the truth, pretty much no matter what.

It is one thing to cite an aphorism, quite another to give an argument. Why is honesty the best policy? We can see why by considering something called the broken leg problem. Suppose you are a social scientist, and you and your colleagues have developed an algorithm for determining whether a given individual will go to the movie theater within the next week. Your algorithm has been painstakingly tweaked over time, and it takes into account a bunch of variables—the subject's age, gender, socio-economic background, where the subject lives, their past movie-going behavior, what they like to watch, the cinemas near their house, what is currently playing at those cinemas, how many hours a week they work, whether they have friends or relatives visiting, the forecasted weather for the coming week, whether their car is in good working order, etc., etc. There are also some weird variables in the algorithm that you wouldn't expect but which make the algorithm more reliable. It takes into account whether the subject ate breakfast three days ago, whether their moon is in Scorpio, and whether they took swimming lessons as a child. You get the point; the algorithm is complex and in many ways counterintuitive. What's more, it works very, very well. If you pick any random individual off the street and feed their information into the algorithm, it gets the right answer 95% of the time. Basically, if the algorithm says that the subject will go to the movie theater, then they will, and if it says they won't, then they won't. Importantly, the algorithm that you and your colleagues have developed is more reliable than any one of you making a judgment without the algorithm. If you or one of your colleagues tries to predict whether a random person will go to the movies in the next week, you're worse than chance; you get the right answer only 45% of the time. All of this (we imagine) has been scientifically verified.

It sure seems like you should always trust the algorithm over your own hunches or educated guesses, right? Well, suppose your job is to predict whether Matilda will go to the movies this week. Here's the catch: Matilda's leg is broken, and you know that there is no broken-leg variable in your algorithm. In other words, you know (or think you know) that (a) whether someone's leg is broken is probably an important factor in determining whether they go to the movies, (b) Matilda's leg is broken, and (c) the algorithm does not take this fact into account. Should you rely on the algorithm to predict Matilda's behavior, or should you ignore the algorithm and make your own judgment? Remember that in the past whenever you have parted ways with the algorithm, you have usually gotten the wrong answer.

The problem with saying that you should part ways with the algorithm is that you already know the algorithm is very reliable. If you decide to ignore the algorithm in making your prediction, then what could your reason possibly be? The obvious answer is that Matilda has a broken leg. But if you can part ways with the algorithm over a broken leg, can you ignore it for other reasons as well? Presumably, yes. And now it looks like you will need a new algorithm—an algorithm to tell you whether you should use the original algorithm. Of course there might be occasions when you think you have good reason to ignore this meta-algorithm too, so you'll need a meta-meta-algorithm to determine whether you should use the meta-algorithm. And the meta-meta-algorithm might not always be reliable ...

To avoid this infinite regress, a good *policy* would be to just follow the original algorithm no matter what. It has proven reliable, and if you try to predict without it, you already know that you're likely to get the wrong answer. More importantly, even when you think you have good reason to part ways with the algorithm, you should probably stick with it anyway. Otherwise, either you'll need to develop an infinite number of meta-algorithms (which is impossible) or you'll start making baseless, arbitrary decisions about when to use the algorithm and when to ignore it. The only sensible option seems to be to make no exceptions to this rule: Use the algorithm to predict a subject's movie-going likelihood.

I trust you see where I'm going with this. Just as it is best to make a policy out of following the algorithm, it is best to make a policy out of telling the truth. If you do not—if you allow for exceptions to truth-telling—you will get morally lost because you won't have any way of determining when you should stick to the rule that says "Tell the truth" and when you should disregard it. If you make an exception to the honesty rule when it comes to your friend's silly hat, will you make an exception when it comes to their silly shoes, or the clothes they plan on wearing to a job interview, or their choice of romantic partner? What about when it comes to even more important life choices? Will you lie in order to spare their feelings even then? If so, you are very likely to hurt your friend with your lying, and that is certainly not moral. To avoid this outcome, it looks like you're going to need another moral rule that will tell you when it is moral to make exceptions to the honesty rule. It is hard to imagine what this second rule would look like and you will need an even more hard-to-imagine third rule to determine when to make exceptions to the second rule, and so on. This regress has all the makings of a moral disaster. You really should make truth telling a *policy*—an exceptionless personal rule. For this reason, you should not lie to people to spare their feelings.

18. Is it ok to ignore your drama-prone friend?

Clarification

Most people have at least one friend whose life seems to be filled with drama. This is the friend who always thinks they are dealing with an earth-shattering tragedy. The pseudo tragedy might concern their love life, other relationships, their job, their grades, their ability to pay the rent, or a host of other things. We all encounter difficulties, but there are some people who seem to be constantly and continuously facing difficulties, in part because they make life much more difficult than it needs to be. I hope you have an idea of the kind of people I'm talking about. If one of these people is a friend of yours, is it morally permissible for you to decide that you just can't deal with them when they again start making mountains out of molehills? Is it ok for you to in effect say, "I really can't talk right now. Let's talk once you get your problems sorted out?"

Con

Either the drama-prone person is your friend or they're not. If you don't talk to them, listen to them, support them, and help them, then they're not really your friend. If, on the other hand, they really are your friend, then you may not ignore them when they are going through tough times. Whatever else we might want to say about the concept of friendship, we have to say at least this: If someone is your friend, then you must care about what they care about. To some extent, you must make their projects and worries your own. If you are not prepared to do this for someone, then they are not a friend. Therefore, no, it is not morally permissible for you to ignore your drama-prone *friend*, though it might be ok for you to ignore a drama-prone person who is not your friend.

Pro

You can be morally obligated to help your drama-prone friend only if your help is likely to be effective. But when you're dealing with the kind of people described in the clarification section, there is no helping them. These people seek out trouble and heartache. There is no helping someone who doesn't want to help themself. For this reason, you are not morally obligated to help your drama-prone friend. Furthermore, just because you ignore your friend during yet another of their "episodes," it doesn't follow that they are not really your friend. Friendship is a two-way street. Yes, you must make some sacrifices for your friends, but your friends must make some sacrifices for you as well. Moreover, friendship does *not* require that you constantly make huge sacrifices. Hence your drama-prone friend should not expect you to listen to them or help them *every time* they face another problem that they have manufactured for themself. Therefore, it is morally permissible for you to ignore your drama-prone friend, at least some of the time.

19. Is it ok to correct other people's grammar?

Clarification

We will assume that the grammar mistake is made by someone who the would-be corrector knows fairly well. We're not talking about running around correcting the grammar of perfect strangers. Neither are we talking about a case in which grammar correction is expected, e.g., when an instructor grades a student's paper or when a parent's child commits an egregious error. (I heard a kid say "gots" instead of "has" the other day. Argh.)

Pro

Not only is it morally *permissible* to correct other people's grammar; in many cases doing so might be morally *obligatory*. The reason is fairly straightforward: The good of correcting the misuse of language far outweighs the bad. To show this, let's do a simple good–bad comparison:

GOOD:
- Future grammar mistakes (of the same kind, at least) are less likely, and hence the expressive power of the language is better safeguarded.
- The friend or acquaintance is likely to become a better communicator going forward, which can save them from future embarrassment and make them more successful in general.

BAD:
- The friend or acquaintance is mildly embarrassed.
- The corrector is mildly uncomfortable.
- Some strain is placed on the relationship between the corrector and correctee.

Some people complain that cost–benefit analyses of real-world, non-financial situations are not very useful because the real world is too complex and the relevant considerations too varied for lists such as those above to help us in determining what should be done. Those people are wrong. Sure, there are cases that don't lend themselves very well to cost–benefit analyses, but some do, and this is one of them, as I will soon show.

You might think that the lists above suggest that it is *not* ok to correct others' grammar because there are more "bads" than "goods." But this would be a mistake. The question is not whether the goods out*number* the bads, but whether the goods out*weigh* the bads. Just as one concrete block might outweigh 1,000 grains of rice, fewer benefits can outweigh more costs. So it is not enough to simply count up the goods and bads; we must also consider how good the goods are and how bad the bads are. In the present case, the two goods are really good, and the three bads aren't all that bad.

Consider the benefits first. The first one is based on a fairly simple idea, which is that we want our language to be capable of expressing our ideas as well as possible. But when grammar mistakes go uncorrected, there is a good chance that our language will be made *less* expressively powerful. I could give you many, many examples of common grammatical errors that have hurt English, but I'll just briefly give three. A fairly well-known mistake is to use the word 'literally' in order to add emphasis, as in "I literally hate grammar mistakes." Here, 'literally' is used to do what 'intensely' or even 'really' could do just as well. That's not such a problem so far, but if 'literally' gets misused this way too often, then we will have no good way of conveying what the word used to convey. Suppose I'm telling you about the time I had a motorcycle accident and I say, "I literally broke my back." Does that mean that actually, truly, *in real life* I broke vertebrae and was put in traction in the hospital? Or does it just mean that I was badly hurt? It's impossible to know ever since people started using 'literally' incorrectly. See? It's irritating.

Another example: Many of my students seem to think that 'i.e.' and 'e.g.' can be used interchangeably. This can cause confusion, in that I sometimes don't know whether they're trying to state a definition or give an example.

One final example: For a long time, the term 'vis-à-vis' in English did *not* mean the same as 'with respect to.' It referred to a particular *kind* of relationship, namely a relationship of opposition. But now that its misuse has become so common, this previously very useful term has lost its specificity. We now have no easy way of expressing what 'vis-à-vis' used to express.

When a language loses its expressive power, that's a bad thing. When you correct people's grammar mistakes, you help to prevent that bad thing from occurring, at least a little bit. And it's good to help to prevent bad things, even if just a little bit.

The second benefit associated with correcting people's grammar is that the person who is corrected will be better off, assuming they take the mini grammar lesson to heart. There are two reasons for thinking the correctee will benefit. First, in learning that how they express themself matters, they will become a better communicator in general. A very large part of living a fulfilling life involves communicating effectively with others in order to inform them about what you believe, what you want, and how they might help you. Since grammar is the set of rules that governs this process of communication, it is better to know the rules than to not.

Second, the fact is that many people—especially people who are likely to be in positions of power, e.g., college professors, employers, and prospective employers—will judge you very poorly if you make grammar mistakes. The pretty obvious conclusion is that you're not doing your friends or acquaintances any favors by not correcting their bad grammar. In fact, you're doing them a disservice by setting them up for future failure.

But what about the costs of correcting someone's grammar? Well, none of them are very severe. Mild embarrassment of the person corrected is ... mild. The discomfort that might be felt by the corrector is also mild. For these reasons, whatever strain might be put on the relationship between corrector and correctee is bound to be minimal. The lesson is that the goods of correcting someone's grammar far outweigh the bads. This shows that you probably *should* correct people's grammar. At the very least, it is permissible for you to do so.

Con

There are two closely related reasons why you shouldn't correct other people's grammar in most cases. The first is based on the basic idea that correcting someone's grammar is disrespectful, and it is immoral to be disrespectful. The second reason is based on scientific findings which suggest that those who correct others' grammar are jerks.

Let us consider the first reason first. When you correct someone's grammar you are in effect declaring, "Even though I understand what you said perfectly well, I now wish to demonstrate my superiority by criticizing the way you said it and by belittling you." Regardless of whether this is the attitude you actually have when you correct people, very often they are going to take it that way. And when you know people are likely to understand your correction that way, you show disrespect if you go ahead and correct anyway. That's just how respect and disrespect work. For example, you might not understand the point of various dress codes in places of worship and you might violate a dress code without *intending* to show disrespect for someone's religion, but if you know about a temple's or church's dress code and you violate it, then you have in fact shown disrespect. Your actions are disrespectful simply because you know that they probably will be interpreted as disrespectful by others. Similarly, since you know that many people will feel disrespected if you correct their grammar, you do in fact disrespect them if you go ahead and correct them anyway, regardless of your intent.

Although I find this line of reasoning persuasive (and so should you), some people might claim just the opposite—that respect actually *requires* you to correct others' grammar. The idea is that to truly respect an intelligent adult is to trust them to be able to take in information (including criticism), process it, make a decision, and act accordingly. The objection is that when you refuse to correct someone's grammar, you show that you do *not* trust them to deal with information, and that isn't respectful, it's *dis*respectful. In other words, it is disrespectful to shield intelligent adults from the truth and that's precisely what you would be doing if you refrain from correcting others' grammar.

The problem with this objection is that it assumes respect and disrespect are related only to our ability to think logically. It ignores the role that emotion plays. Maybe we can safely focus solely on logical reasoning if we're trying to figure out how to respect an android, but when we want to know how to respect real people living in the real world, we must take into account their emotions because humans are emotional creatures. In order to respect someone, it is not enough to consider only how they might "process information." You must also consider how your actions might make them *feel*. Most of the time, correcting a person's grammar will make them feel crappy, and that is why doing so is disrespectful.

The lesson is that when you go around correcting the way others speak, you act like a jerk. This brings us to the second reason why you shouldn't correct other people's grammar: There is scientific evidence that if you are the sort of person who judges others on the basis of their grammar, then you are in fact a jerk. In a recent study, subjects were asked to read email messages that contained spelling and grammar mistakes. They were asked to evaluate the message writers' level of intelligence and personality. Predictably, some subjects seemed to judge people harshly on the basis of grammar mistakes, while other subjects did not. Experimenters then gave the subjects a standard personality inventory designed to measure their personality on the "Big Five" parameters: openness to experience, conscientiousness, introversion/extroversion, agreeableness, and neuroticism. Those subjects who judged the message writers harshly on the basis of their grammar mistakes tended to be close-minded, conscientious, introverted, and disagreeable. Think about that combination of personality traits. I can't take the space here to explain these factors in any detail, but isn't it pretty clear that someone who is close-minded, tends to act out of duty, does not want to engage socially, and who places their self-interest above getting along well with others is the walking definition of the word 'jerk'? Well, that is precisely the kind of person that grammar fascists tend to be. Don't be that kind of person. Don't correct other people's grammar.

Now, someone might object that if you have a jerky personality that might not be your fault. It's not like we choose where we're going to fall on the openness or agreeability spectrum. And if it is a certain set of personality traits that causes you to correct others' grammar, then how can you be said to be doing anything immoral? It seems like you're just doing what your personality makes you do, and you can't be blamed for *that*. We don't blame the introvert for being introverted or the neurotic for having neurosis. Likewise, we shouldn't blame the grammar corrector for the personality traits that make them a grammar corrector. And when we should not blame, we should not talk of immorality. Right?

Wrong. Like the other objection considered in this essay, this response assumes an overly simplistic view of humans and the way they interact with the world. Specifically, the current objection assumes that the connection between personality and behavior is a one-way street. But that's incorrect. Of course it is true that our personalities influence our actions, but it is also true that we can change our personalities by choosing to act in particular ways. For example, introverts can make themselves a little less introverted by forcing themselves to socially engage more with others. Their ability to make themselves more extroverted might be limited and individual differences can also have an important effect, but most introverts can make themselves at least a *little bit* less introverted by making it a point to *behave* more like an extrovert. Now, whether an introvert should *want* to be more extroverted is a good question. But if what makes you want to correct others' grammar includes a combination of close-mindedness and disagreeableness, you should probably want to diminish those traits. Just as introverts can make themselves less introverted by acting like extroverts, grammar jerks can make themselves less jerky by not correcting other people's grammar. None of us should be grammar jerks and hence we should not correct others' grammar.

20. Is it ok to post about controversial topics on social media?

Clarification

We're talking about posting comments or links that show where you stand on a controversial political or social issue, when you know full well that many of the people who follow you on social media disagree (perhaps very strongly) with your point of view. For example, is it ok for you to routinely call your friends' and family's attention to places on the web where it is claimed that climate change is a lie when you know that many of your friends and family think otherwise and are very concerned about the effects of global warming?

Con

The main reason why you shouldn't post controversial items on social media is simple: no good can come from it, and it can do damage to your relationships. Controversial topics are controversial because people tend to have strong opinions about them that they are very unlikely to give up as a result of anything you link to on social media. So your friends on social media who already disagree with you are not going to change their minds on the basis of a link you have posted or a comment you've made. Furthermore, even if all of your "friends" on social media agreed with your stance on a controversial topic, it wouldn't be clear why you were posting about it in the first place! Are you trying to convince them of something they already believe? That's weird.

Consider this argument:

(1) When you post controversial items on social media, you either (a) needlessly irritate people or (b) tell people things they already believe.

(2) If you needlessly irritate people, then you act like a jerk.
(3) If you tell people things they already believe, then you do not accomplish anything.

---

(4) When you post controversial items on social media, you either act like a jerk or you accomplish nothing.
(5) For any action, if it either involves acting like a jerk or accomplishing nothing, then you should not do that action.

---

(6) You should not post controversial items on social media.

The first idea behind the first premise is that anyone who disagrees with you will be irritated by your post. Furthermore, there is very good reason to think that anyone who disagrees with you is very unlikely to change their mind simply because you have made the post. This is why I say that the poster of controversial items *needlessly* irritates people. If you had a realistic expectation that you might change Aunt Sue's mind about which political party is the right one to vote for, then your post might irritate Sue, but you wouldn't be *needlessly* irritating her if you had a good chance of bringing Aunt Sue around to your way of thinking. Unfortunately, Aunt Sue is very unlikely to change her mind on the basis of what you do on social media.

The second idea behind the first premise is that if Aunt Sue, for example, already believes as you do, then there's just no reason to tell her that she ought to vote for this or that particular party.

The second premise is obviously true. We might even *define* a jerk as someone who needlessly irritates people.

The third premise might be called into question. You might think that you do accomplish something by "preaching to the choir." Maybe there is a sense of solidarity that arises between friends who continuously tell each other that they're correct on some issue. Maybe friends feel better about each other in these circumstances, maybe their relationships are strengthened.

Whether premise (3) is justified depends on results from social science. So it is difficult to say whether we should accept premise (3) as it stands. For now, though, I just want to suggest that even if *maybe* something good is accomplished when friends tell each other that their opinions are right, this benefit is outweighed by the potential bad done when your friends do not agree with you. In other words, if you are sure that all of your social media friends agree with the point of view you advocate on a controversial topic, then post away. But if you know or think there is a good chance that even one person who follows you on social media will be irritated by your post, then you should not make the post.

In response to both premise (2) and premise (3) someone might suggest that *they*—the poster—gains some benefit by posting controversial stuff. This is a challenge to premise (2) because it is a challenge to the idea that irritating your friends with your political views is needless. It is a challenge to premise (3) because it is a challenge to the idea that when you speak (or post) you accomplish something only if your speech (or posting) has some kind of effect on your audience. Perhaps the speaker can benefit from her own speech, and hence maybe preaching to the choir can indeed accomplish something.

I leave it to the reader to decide whether this objection to premises (2) and (3) is a good one. But again I will suggest that in the case of controversial social media posts, the bad is very likely to outweigh the good. And remember that you are only one person—your feelings and well-being count for one, but only for one. Aunt Sue's feelings and well-being count just as much as yours.

In the above argument, (4) follows from (1) through (3), so you can't object to (4) without objecting to one of (1) through (3).

I'm not sure how to back up premise (5) since it seems so obviously true to me. If the only possible outcomes of what you do are that people get irritated or nothing at all happens, then you pretty clearly act immorally.

It follows that (6) is true. You should not post about controversial topics on social media. It's irritating, pointless, or both.

Pro

The problem with the argument presented in the con essay isn't a problem with this or that premise. The argument is fine, but it doesn't show what it needs to show. The reason is that the argument is all about what you should or should not do, but the word "should" is ambiguous. On the one hand, there is the moral meaning of "should." On this reading, to say that you should not do x is to say that it is immoral for you to do x. On the other hand, there is the practical meaning of "should." On this reading, to say that you should not do x is to say that it is a bad idea to do x or that it isn't wise to do x. For example, if I say that you should not starve your children, I'm using the moral "should." I'm saying that it would be flat-out morally wrong for you to starve your children. If I say that you should not take twelve courses in one term, I'm not saying that it would be morally wrong for you to take twelve courses. I'm just saying that it probably wouldn't be a good idea to do so. Taking twelve courses wouldn't be good for you.

In the con essay, the conclusion of the main argument is: "You should not post controversial items on social media." The "should" here seems to be the pragmatic should. It might not be a good idea for you to constantly post controversial things on social media, but that hardly shows that it is morally wrong for you to do so. As far as I can tell, the con argument establishes only the practical should, not the moral should. Our question is a question about what is or is not *moral*, and hence the argument in the con essay does not really address our question.

There are two principles that you probably already accept and that suggest it is *morally* ok to for you to post controversial things on social media. These principles are the freedom of speech and the freedom of association. Now, it is very important to distinguish these principles as *legal* principles and the *legal* rights associated with them from the principles understood as *moral* principles with accompanying *moral* rights. I am not making any legal claim, and I am not basing my argument on the US Constitution or any other legal document. It is a mistake for an American to say that they have the right to make controversial posts on social media because the First Amendment guarantees them that right. The Constitution doesn't have anything to do with whether you have the moral right to speak your mind. It merely says that the *government* cannot *legally* stifle your speech. So forget any argument that makes use of any legal protections. Such an argument would be a bad one.

Still, we can and should ask why many people think that legal protections of speech and association are important. Isn't it because they also think that the principles of freedom of speech and freedom of association are *morally* important, even outside of legal contexts?

The whole reason entire societies have decided to encode freedom of speech and freedom of association in their legal systems is that entire societies think it is morally good when people are able to say what they want to say and morally good when people are able to interact with the people who they want to interact with. Although the principles that are relevant to the present question are not legal principles, they are closely related to legal principles. Now ask yourself whether you agree with the moral versions of these principles. I'm betting that you do.

If freedom of speech is morally good, then it is morally permissible for people to express themselves however they see fit, as long as their expression doesn't cause immediate harm. If freedom of association is morally good, then it is morally permissible for people to express themselves *to* whomever they wish. And now we have an argument:

> **(1)** If freedom of speech and freedom of association are morally good, then it is morally permissible for people to say whatever they like to whomever they like.
>
> **(2)** Freedom of speech and freedom of association are morally good.
>
> ---
>
> **(3)** It is morally permissible for people to say what they like to whomever they like.
>
> **(4)** To post controversial topics on social media is to say what you want to whomever you want.
>
> ---
>
> **(5)** It is morally permissible for you to post controversial topics on social media.

21. Is it ok to borrow something without asking?

Clarification

Suppose Tim is dogsitting for his friend David, who is out of town for a couple of weeks. Twice a day, Tim takes David's dog for a walk and feeds her. Occasionally he waters David's plants and generally takes care of things around David's house. Further suppose Tim decides to do some work around his own house and realizes that he needs an electric drill. He also realizes that David has a drill that he could easily borrow. If Tim were to borrow the drill, he would take great care with it and return it to David's house before David returns. Tim also has very good reason to think that if he were to ask David to borrow the drill, David would happily lend it to him. Is it morally permissible for Tim to borrow the drill?

Pro

It is morally permissible for Tim to borrow the drill for the simple reason that if he were to borrow it, no harm would be done. If you know that an action will not cause any harm to anyone, then the action is morally permissible. Therefore, it is morally permissible for Tim to borrow the drill.

There is the further question of whether Tim is morally obligated to tell David afterwards that he borrowed his drill, but just to keep things simple, let's suppose that if he were to borrow the drill, he would not tell David that he did so. With this detail of the story in place, it becomes even more clear that Tim's action would cause no harm to David, himself, or anyone else. That is why it is morally ok for him to borrow David's property without asking.

Con

A moral slippery slope argument is an argument in which it is claimed that if we say that a certain action or policy has a certain moral status (e.g., is morally permissible) for a particular set of reasons, then those same reasons will make us fall down a conceptual slope and force us to say that some other action has that same moral status, even though we don't think that the second action has that status. The conclusion of a moral slippery slope argument is that the reasons given for thinking the first action has the moral status attributed to it must be mistaken.

I know that's a mouthful so maybe an example would help. Suppose Denise thinks it's morally permissible to eat meat. Mysti, who is a fervent vegetarian, disagrees. Mysti argues against Denise's position with a slippery slope argument; she says that if it is ok for humans to farm and eat other animals such as chickens, pigs, and cows, then it is also ok for humans to farm and eat other humans. Mysti says that it would be wrong for us to farm and eat other humans (obviously), so it is wrong for us to farm and eat other animals. Mysti concludes that there must be something wrong with Denise's reasons for thinking meat-eating is ok.

Clearly Mysti's argument is a bad argument. The reason it's a bad argument is that Mysti has failed to show that Denise's reasons for thinking meat-eating is ok would also suggest that human-eating is ok. Perhaps the arguments for the permissibility of meat-eating are not very good, but Mysti's argument just doesn't show that. Denise might have all sorts of reasons for thinking that farming and eating chickens is ok, but farming and eating humans is not. In other words, Denise's justification for meat-eating might not (and probably doesn't) justify human-eating.

A good number of moral slippery slope arguments are fallacious in just the way that Mysti's is. But not *all* slippery slope arguments are fallacious. So how can you tell whether a slippery slope argument is fallacious or reasonable? The answer is that with a fallacious slippery slope, no reason is given for thinking that we will really fall down the slope. The reasoning that is the target of the slippery slope argument is ignored or misrepresented. Mysti doesn't pay any attention to whatever reasons Denise has for her position on carnivorism, and that is why her slippery slope argument doesn't work. In contrast, a reasonable slippery slope argument is one in which the target reasons are acknowledged and in which it is *argued* that those reasons lead us to an implausible position. In other words, a reasonable slippery slope argument actually gives us a reason to think that we will fall down the slope.

Now, what on earth does all of this have to do with borrowing things without asking? Well, there is a reasonable, non-fallacious slippery slope argument that can be used against the argument presented in the pro essay. I have said a bit about slippery slope arguments and what makes them good or bad because I do not want others to say anything like, "But that's a just a slippery slope argument." Even if many or even most slippery slope arguments are fallacious, it does not follow that all are, and the argument I'm about to give is not fallacious. So, without further ado, here it is.

The reasoning in the pro essay justifies straight-up stealing. Stealing is immoral. Therefore, the reasoning used in the pro essay is faulty.

To convince you that this slippery slope argument is not fallacious, I must now explain how and why the pro essay argument would justify stealing. Suppose that Tim, in need of a drill, knows David has several in his garage. Further suppose that Tim knows that if he were to just take one of the older drills, David wouldn't even notice. Would it be ok for Tim to just swipe the drill (or to take a $5 bill he finds buried in a kitchen drawer, or to just help himself to a can of beans in David's cupboard)? The answer, clearly enough, is no. Stealing is wrong. But if Tim knows that David will not notice the missing drill (or cash or beans), then Tim's theft will not *harm* David or anyone else. (You can make up a lot of farfetched stories in which the absence of the old drill somehow manages to harm David, but if you did this, then you'd be missing the point.) Thus, if we use the principle that says "no harm, no foul," as the pro essay does, then we would justify stealing. That, however, isn't really possible. Stealing is wrong even if the victim doesn't realize he has been stolen from. It follows that the "no harm, no foul" principle is false. Since the argument in the pro essay obviously depends very heavily on this principle, we should reject the argument.

Still, just because the argument in the pro essay fails, that doesn't mean that it is wrong for Tim to borrow David's drill without asking.

Showing that someone's argument doesn't work doesn't show that the conclusion of their argument is false. But in this case it is fairly easy to turn the criticism of the pro argument into a good con argument. The reason why it's easy is that it seems like the *only* way to justify borrowing without asking is to rely on the "no harm, no foul" principle and, as we have seen, that principle is false. Here, then, is the argument that it is not morally permissible to borrow things without asking:

(1) If it is morally permissible to borrow things without asking, then the "no harm, no foul" principle is true.

(2) If the "no harm, no foul" principle is true, then it is morally permissible to steal anything that wouldn't be missed by its owner.

(3) It is not morally permissible to steal something just because it wouldn't be missed by its owner.

---

(4) It is not morally permissible to borrow things without asking.

22. Is it ok to date your friend's ex?

Clarification

The question is fairly straightforward, I think. Your friend was going out with someone. They aren't any longer. Is it morally permissible for you to go out with that person?

Pro

(1) If it is morally permissible for two people to consent to date, then it is morally permissible for you to date your friend's former significant other.
(2) It is morally permissible for two people to consent to date.

---

(3) It is morally permissible for you to date your friend's former significant other.

Con

(1) It is not morally permissible to betray a friend.
(2) To date your friend's former significant other is to betray your friend.

---

(3) It is not morally permissible to date your friend's former significant other.

Option 3—It depends.

(1) If it is morally permissible for two people to consent to date, then it is morally permissible for you to date your friend's former significant other, but *only if* you do not lie about the relationship.

(2) It is morally permissible for two people to consent to date.

(3) It is not morally permissible to betray a friend.

(4) If you date your friend's former significant other *without first getting your friend's blessing*, then you betray your friend.

---

(5) It is morally permissible to date your friend's former significant other, but *only if* you (a) do not lie about the relationship and (b) you get your friend's blessing first.

23. Is it ok to ghost someone?

Clarification

Most people are probably familiar with the phenomenon of ghosting. To ghost someone is to abruptly stop communication with them, without warning. This takes the form of not responding to texts, app messages, phone calls, or emails. There is some evidence that the term originated in the context of dating, and especially online dating and flirtatious behavior on social media. Over time, people started using the term to refer to *any* case in which communication is expected but never comes, e.g., when someone is ghosted by a potential employer after a job interview. But let us focus on the original sense and ask whether it is morally permissible to ghost someone with whom you are in a romantic or potentially romantic relationship.

Con

Ghosting is wrong for two reasons. First, it is very disrespectful. Second, it has the potential to do much harm to the person ghosted.

Imagine you have a coworker who you don't get along with very well. Suppose that, for whatever reason, there is "bad blood" between the two of you. It would be wrong for either of you to show disrespect to the other, even though you don't like each other too much. After all, liking someone and showing them the respect that all persons deserve are completely different things. Unless one of you has done something really, really bad, respect is still required. Now imagine that your coworker starts to ignore you entirely. When you ask them a question, they act as if you haven't said anything at all. They don't communicate things to you that they do communicate to others. They don't so much as acknowledge your existence. That would be wrong because it is disrespectful.

The analogy with ghosting is pretty obvious. Just ignoring someone who has reason to expect that you will *not* ignore them is not ok.

If it's wrong in the case of coworkers, then it is especially wrong in the case of ghosting a potential romantic partner. At least with the coworkers it is understood that neither likes the other. In the case of ghosting, the ghoster might not dislike the ghostee. Clearly, if it is disrespectful and hence wrong to just ignore someone you hate, then it is also disrespectful and hence wrong to just ignore someone you don't hate. So, ghosting is wrong.

Even more importantly, ghosting someone is likely to cause them harm. Anyone who is ghosted is quite reasonably going to think that there must be something about them that the ghoster doesn't like. That's already kinda hard to take, but what makes ghosting doubly difficult to endure is that the ghostee doesn't even *know* what caused them to be ghosted. It's one thing to know that someone isn't interested in you because they think you're arrogant or too sensitive or not considerate enough or not smart enough, or whatever. It's quite another to know that someone isn't interested in you and to also deal with the agony of not knowing what it is that they don't like about you. In the first case, you at least have the option of thinking something like, "She says I'm arrogant, but that's because she often misunderstands what I'm trying to say." Or, you could acknowledge that you can sometimes be a little arrogant and either make an effort to fix this character flaw or just decide to live with it. But in the case where you don't even know what it is that the other person doesn't like about you, these options don't exist. That's what makes ghosting doubly bad, and it is the main reason why it is wrong to ghost someone.

People ghost others because it's just easier and because it causes *them*—the ghoster—less discomfort than telling the ghostee that the relationship is over. But if that is your reason for ghosting someone, you are a moral coward. Morality sometimes requires you to do things that you would rather not do or things which are bound to make you uncomfortable. If you opt for the easy way out instead of doing the right thing, that's pretty bad.

Pro

The analogy between the disrespectful coworker and the ghoster is informative, but not in the way that the author of the con essay thinks it is. There is a very important *disanalogy* between ignoring your coworker and ghosting someone on a dating app. The difference is this: In the case of the coworkers there is an expectation—a starting assumption—that they must put their differences aside and interact with each other as needed to do their jobs. This expectation is quite reasonable and the person who violates it does indeed act disrespectfully. But there just isn't any similar expectation in the context of contemporary dating or flirting. Everyone knows, going in, that there is a possibility they'll be ghosted, so it is not disrespectful or wrong to ghost someone.

Consider again a pair of coworkers. Let's use the example of me and one of my professor colleagues. It would be disrespectful and wrong for me to come into the department one day and punch my colleague in the face. Obviously. But suppose my colleague and I have a shared interest in amateur boxing. So we decide to meet up at a boxing gym and spar. At some point I hit them hard in the face. Would *that* be disrespectful or wrong? Clearly not, since there is an expectation—a starting assumption—that when you box with someone you're likely to get hit by them. My colleague has agreed to take on the risk of getting hit when they decide to step into the ring with me. *This* is the right kind of analogy with ghosting. When you decide to use a dating app or otherwise try to find a romantic partner, you take on the risk of being ghosted. For this reason, the potential romantic partner who suddenly cuts off all communication acts no more disrespectfully than the boxer who punches their opponent in the face. Everyone understands that ghosting is a risk when you try to date, just as everyone understands that getting hit in the face is a risk when you try to box. This understanding is enough to eliminate the concern of acting disrespectfully.

But what about the harm issue raised in the con essay? Isn't the ghostee harmed by the ghoster? Maybe, but not in a way that makes the harm immoral. And this is an important lesson: It is not *always* wrong to do needless harm. To see why, all you have to do is again consider my colleague and me. I'm very likely to cause them harm—physical harm—when I hit them in the face in the boxing ring. But again, that's what they've signed up for, so it is difficult to see how the harm I do to them is wrong. And now make the analogy: When you enter onto the dating scene, you sign up for dealing with all the behavior that is expected and commonplace on the dating scene, and that includes being harmed by ghosting. The harm done to you is not wrong. Furthermore, the alternative to someone ghosting you—telling you why they want to call things off—might do *more* harm than if they were to ghost you. Imagine that someone tells you that they don't want to pursue a relationship because they think you're very boring. Surely *that* would make you feel way worse than not knowing why they want to end things.

It is important to add that shared expectations can also eliminate concerns about moral cowardice. It *would* be cowardly for me to punch my colleague when they don't expect it, e.g., at a department meeting, but it is not cowardly for me to punch them in the face when we're boxing. If everyone agrees that one way of ending a relationship is via ghosting, then it is not cowardly to ghost someone. And if ghosting is often the easiest way for people to end relationships, then why shouldn't they use that method?

V. Children

Is it ok to ...

24. Is it ok to swear in the presence of children?

Clarification

The children referred to here are children you have a close relationship with, such as your own children, your younger siblings, your nieces or nephews, or the children of close friends. The kind of swearing we're talking about is on the more vulgar or extreme end of the swearing spectrum. We're not talking about "darn" or "shucks," we're talking about "shit," "fuck," "dickhead," etc.

Pro

I have never understood why people think swearing, cursing, cussing, or whatever you want to call it, is bad in the first place. Like many other words, swear words are used to convey thoughts and emotions. Ironically though, the fact that people think swearing is bad—the fact that swearing is taboo—is what gives swear words their power. Even though it doesn't make a lot of sense to think that swearing is bad, the fact that people think it is bad is what gives swear words their unique ability to express anger, exasperation, disgust, or whatever. That's weird and interesting, but again, I can't for the life of me figure out why people have decided that certain acoustic blasts coming out of people's mouths are bad in and of themselves, whereas other acoustic blasts are fine. In mixed company it's ok to say "Shoot, that really hurt!" but it's not ok to say "God-damn motherfucking son of a bitch, that fucking hurt!" I don't see why. The swear words just add color to the expression.

If there is no reason to think that swearing is immoral (and there isn't), then there is no reason why you shouldn't swear in front of children. Generally, if an activity is not immoral, then it is not immoral to do it in the presence of kids. There are some exceptions, of course. It's not immoral to have sex, but you might not want to do that in front of a six-year-old. Still, the generalization holds as a generalization, so unless there is something special about swearing in front of children that makes it different from eating or sleeping or talking in front of children, there isn't anything morally wrong with it.

Another consideration is that the children who are close to you *are going to hear swear words anyway*. Every kid hears swear words eventually. I can't even imagine a child growing up in the English-speaking world not hearing the gold standard of cursing—"fuck" or one of its variants—long before they turn six. This is true whether their parents swear or not. What, then, could you possibly be protecting children from when you refuse to swear in front of them? Nothing.

Furthermore, a lot of people don't know how to swear properly, so if you do swear, you might as well model good swearing practice for the children around you. You may know people or at least heard other people who overuse "fuck," especially in its adjectival and adverbial forms. Everything is fuckin' this or fuckin' that for them, even when nothing they are saying is particularly emotion-laden or even interesting. Example: "Yeah, I fuckin' went to fuckin' school today, and my fuckin' teacher was fuckin' out sick. We had a fuckin' substitute." This is bad practice not because it is immoral, but because it makes the speaker sound like an idiot. If your children decide to use swear words themselves, you don't want this idiotic form of swearing to serve as the model for them, and hence you should model the proper use of swear words. (It's not so clear what you should do if you yourself do not typically swear. That's tough, but my purpose here is only to show that it is morally *permissible* to swear in front of children, not that you have a moral *obligation* to do so.)

To summarize, there are three reasons why it is morally permissible to swear in the presence of children: First, there is nothing wrong with swearing in the first place. Second, refusing to swear in front of children does not protect them from anything. Third, it is better to model good swearing for the children close to you than to allow others to teach them to swear badly.

Con

It is agreed that in general there is nothing wrong with adults swearing if they want to. Of all the moral rules that a lot of people accept, the prohibition on swearing is one of the most puzzling. The pro essay gets that right, but it gets the modeling issue completely wrong. When you swear in front of children, you are probably doing something morally wrong, not because you somehow harm the children at the time when you swear, but rather because your swearing will harm them later. The reason is that even if you're an excellent swearer, young children close to you probably don't have the wherewithal to understand how to swear well or when swearing is appropriate. In other words, it's not possible to serve as a *good* model of someone who uses swear words. You can serve only as a *bad* model for your kids, and that is why you should not swear in front of them.

I have never refrained from swearing in front of my daughter, even when she was very young. But I should have refrained. In this way I am a bad father. I know this to be the case because of two episodes, which I will now share with you. The first occurred when my daughter was about three years old. She was in her room, getting ready for bed, and I called to her from the bottom of the stairs to ask whether she had brushed her teeth. She yelled down, "Not yet. I'm just putting on my fucking pajamas." I found her response funny, but it also serves as evidence that I should not have sworn in her presence. The second event involved the kids' show "Yo Gabba Gabba!," which my daughter used to watch pretty frequently. The intro song for the show is very catchy, and my daughter would sing along with it. One day as I was listening to her sing the song, I realized that she had fallen prey to a mondegreen. (A mondegreen is a mishearing of lyrics that changes their meaning.) In the song, the characters are introduced, and one line is "Foofa! She's pink and happy." My daughter was singing, "Foofa! She's fucking happy." When I told her that I thought she had gotten the lyric wrong, she argued with me and insisted that the "fucking happy" lyric was correct. Again hilarious, but again proof that parents probably shouldn't swear in front of their children.

What these two events demonstrate is that although I curse like a champ, I did not serve as a good swearing model for my daughter. This in turn might hurt her in the future, for at least two reasons. First, when she hears me swear (all the time), she is more likely to think that using swear words is perfectly normal and she will miss the fact that swearing is taboo. The evidence for this is that she thought it perfectly normal for a kids' TV show to freely use the phrase "fucking happy." Her lack of knowledge of the social prohibition on casual swearing could get her in some trouble. She might swear in the wrong situation. Of course *I* understand that it would probably be a bad idea to curse like a sailor in a job interview, but does *she* understand that it would probably be a bad idea to swear on her first day at a new school? Because I have modeled casual swearing for her, and because there is in fact a social taboo on casual swearing in many contexts, she is much more likely to swear in a way that will make others think badly of her. In this way I have harmed my daughter.

The second way in which my swearing might negatively affect my daughter is that although I know when the use of swear words adds color and when their use would make me sound like a philistine, it's not clear that my daughter does. The evidence for this is that she thought it appropriate to cheerfully report that she was putting on her "fucking pajamas." That's swearing like a philistine. She didn't understand how swear words are supposed to work. Hence, my swearing in front of her makes it more likely that she will swear in a way that will make others think she's kinda dumb, and that would harm her as well.

Take it from a bad dad. It is unlikely that you will serve as a good swearing model for the children close to you. If you serve as a bad model, you are likely to cause future harm to those children. Obviously enough, it is wrong to cause needless harm to kids. Therefore, it is morally wrong to swear in front of them.

25. Is it ok to discipline other people's children?

Clarification

The question is about disciplining children who are strangers to you. We are not asking about disciplining children who you are in charge of in your capacity as a babysitter, teacher, daycare worker, etc. We are asking about disciplining the children of strangers, not the children of friends or family. The question is not about how children should or shouldn't be disciplined in the first place. Draw the line between discipline and child abuse wherever you like, but understand that the question is about disciplining and (obviously) not about abusing other people's children.

You may have had the following experience (I certainly have). You're at a restaurant. A young family is seated at a table nearby, except that the children aren't actually "seated." Instead, they are running around the restaurant, crawling under tables, and generally annoying other patrons, including you. The parents seem to be oblivious to their children's bad behavior. They either don't notice or don't care. Is it morally permissible for you to say a few stern words to the children as they run past your table?

Pro

The reason it is morally permissible to discipline other people's children is that, assuming the discipline is appropriate, you are likely to make the world a better place, and unless there is some significant countervailing reason for you *not* to discipline others' children, you cannot possibly be faulted for making the world a better place. Let's unpack this sentence a bit. First, what is "appropriate discipline" when we're talking about other people's children? We'll understand "appropriate discipline" this way: your disciplining of a parent's child is appropriate if it would be appropriate for the parent to discipline the child in a similar way. Second, what is this talk about "making the world a better place?" I don't mean anything grandiose here. We're not talking about curing cancer. I just mean that if you are successful in getting children to stop annoying people, then that is a net positive; things are better than they would have been if you had not disciplined the children.

Finally, what would a "significant countervailing reason" be? In some situations, it might be immoral to make the world a better place, if doing so would require you to do something that is morally wrong in and of itself. To take an extreme example, suppose that your neighbor is so irritating that the world would be a better place if he didn't exist. It would probably still be wrong for you to kill him, because murdering your neighbor is pretty morally bad, in and of itself. When it comes to disciplining other people's children, even if doing so would make the world a better place, it could still be an immoral action if there is something about the disciplining that is morally bad in and of itself.

So what I'm asking you to agree to is this: If all three of the following conditions are met, it is morally permissible for you to discipline other people's children if:

(1) It would be morally permissible for the children's parents to discipline the children in the same way.
(2) Disciplining the children would result in a net positive.
(3) There is nothing about disciplining other people's children that makes it bad in and of itself.

If, in the restaurant case, all three conditions are met, then it is morally permissible for you to say something to the little brats. And all three conditions are met in the restaurant case. Therefore, it is morally permissible for you to do what the children's parents should be doing and discipline the kids.

The only possible ways to try to counter this argument are to (a) object to one of the conditions, (b) argue that another condition needs to be added, or (c) argue that one of the conditions is not met in the restaurant case. I must say that I don't see how (a) or (b) are plausible options. At the very least, anyone who disagrees with me and pursues option (a) or (b) is going to have a lot of arguing to do. This leaves option (c). But what condition would the objector say is not met? As far as I can tell, the only condition that a reasonable person might think is not satisfied in the restaurant case is (3). In other words, the objector might say that there is something intrinsically bad about disciplining other people's children.

Presumably, it is permissible for people to discipline their own children. In fact, people have an *obligation* to discipline their children. So if there is something bad about disciplining other people's children, there must be something about the fact that they are *other people's* children that makes it bad. But what could that something be? I agree that people are generally more hesitant to discipline other people's children than their own, but the reason is that we generally shy away from confrontation. If you discipline another person's child, the parent might feel that you're in effect criticizing their parenting. They might get angry with you. But that doesn't show that there is anything *wrong* with you disciplining their child. At best it shows that the prospect of disciplining their child might make you feel a tad uncomfortable. It might also make you feel uncomfortable to admonish someone who cuts in line at the bank, but it wouldn't be *immoral* for you to do so.

If discomfort doesn't make it wrong for you to discipline others' children, then what does make it wrong? I'm honestly asking here. Presumably everyone agrees that children are not property. So disciplining a stranger's child is not like borrowing something from them without asking. Presumably it's not wrong because you are criticizing other people's parenting. In a situation like the restaurant case, their parenting *should* be criticized. Presumably it's not wrong because you have no business meddling in other people's private affairs. In a situation like the restaurant case, their affairs are not private; that's why it is possible for you to discipline the children in the first place.

I conclude that there is no reason to think that condition (3) isn't met in the restaurant case. It is met, as are conditions (1) and (2). If you meet all three conditions, then it is morally permissible for you to discipline someone else's children, and hence it would be morally permissible for you to discipline the kids in the restaurant case.

Con

I have a vivid childhood memory of being disciplined by someone other than my parents. I was probably about six years old. My parents took my brother and me to a baseball game. Suddenly, the woman sitting in front of me turned around and said, somewhat sternly, "Do you mind not kicking my seat? Thank you!" and then turned back around. I had been absentmindedly swinging my legs as I sat, and was occasionally making contact with the woman's seat. Her words floored me, even though she hadn't said them in a particularly mean way. My mom whispered to me, "Were you kicking her seat?" I nodded, trying not to cry. My parents didn't say anything more about it and we watched the rest of the game. But I couldn't enjoy it. For some reason, the woman's admonishment made me feel really awful. I'm sure that if my mom or dad had noticed what I was doing, they would have told me to stop kicking the seat. If that had happened, I would have simply obeyed and forgotten the whole thing within moments. That it was a stranger who disciplined me made me feel like I had done something really, really bad. In the days that followed, I would think about the episode without wanting to. The memory of the woman admonishing me would just hit me, and I felt bad all over again. I am now old, and I *still* get a kinda crappy feeling thinking about what happened.

The point of this story is that the pro essay entirely misses what is bad about disciplining other people's children. The conditions that are laid out in the pro essay are in fact the correct, conditions. I agree that it is morally permissible for you to discipline other people's children if:

(1) It would be morally permissible for the children's parents to discipline the children in the same way.
(2) Disciplining the children would result in a net positive.
(3) There is nothing about disciplining other people's children that makes it bad in and of itself.

Right, but what the pro essay misses is that condition (2) is very often not met. I might even go so far as to say that (2) is *usually* not met. The reason is that the children who get disciplined are likely to feel really crappy about it. When we want to know whether an action results in a net positive or whether an action makes the world a better place, it's true that we must take into account the number of people affected by the action and whether they are affected positively or negatively. And it is true that in the restaurant case a large number of people (most of the patrons) will be positively affected if you discipline the kids who are running around. It is also true that only a small number of people (the children themselves) will be negatively affected by you meting out some discipline. These are not the only relevant considerations, however. Also important is *how* positively or *how* negatively people are affected. The *amount* of positivity or negativity produced also matters. One person feeling a lot worse can outweigh many people feeling slightly better. Since children can be very negatively affected when disciplined by strangers, the restaurant case is likely to be a situation where you would do more harm than good by disciplining the children. Maybe the children would just shrug off your stern words and not be too bothered by them, but maybe they are sensitive children who, like the six-year-old Brian, would feel very badly. Since you don't know, and since the inconvenience you and the other patrons are enduring is very minimal, it is best not to try to discipline the kids in the restaurant.

Ironically, even though the pro essay is an essay about how children should be treated, it does not adequately take into account how children are affected by the treatment in question. Even if condition (3) is met—there is nothing *intrinsically* or *especially* bad about the very act of disciplining other people's children—it is still usually wrong to do so because the good usually does not outweigh the bad. Again, it is condition (2) that the restaurant discipliner doesn't meet, not (3).

Someone might object by saying that it is very odd that children tend to feel so much worse when disciplined by strangers, and that they wouldn't feel so much worse if we lived in a society where it was more common to discipline children who are not your own. If we took to heart the idea that we're all in this together (and we should), then we would be disciplining other people's children all the time, and our children would be disciplined by strangers all the time. Kids would think of being disciplined by a stranger in much the same way that they think of being disciplined by their parents. This objection concludes that the problem isn't really with disciplining other people's children per se, but rather with our overly individualistic society that makes its members feel alienated from each other.

There is indeed something to this objection, but it ignores another aspect of the explanation for why children feel worse when strangers discipline them. If you are a kid with even halfway decent parents, then when they discipline you, you understand that they are not doing it out of malice. You understand that they love you, that although they are disciplining you now, they will hug you later. You certainly do not have that understanding when it is a stranger who disciplines you. You do not feel any love from the stranger and it *does* seem like the stranger doesn't like you too much (even though the strange adult might not dislike you at all). I'm pretty sure that this is part of the explanation for why some kids feel worse when strangers discipline them than when their own parents do. Furthermore, it is difficult to see how this phenomenon could be avoided when you discipline other people's children, since it's just true that you don't love the kids you're disciplining (any more than you "love" all of your fellow humans) and it's just true that the kids know this fact. Because it is impossible for you to overcome the stranger factor when disciplining other people's children, you probably shouldn't, at least in situations such as the restaurant case.

26. Is it ok to lie to children about Santa Claus?

Clarification

I hate to break it to you, but Santa Claus doesn't exist. Yet millions of (mostly Christian) parents around the world lie to their children and tell them that he does exist and that if they're good he will deliver presents to them. Many go to great lengths to perpetuate the lie. Is it morally permissible for parents to behave this way? We could ask the same question about the Easter Bunny, the Tooth Fairy, or Hanukkah Harry, but Santa Claus is the best example.

Pro

Here is an argument that uses several independent premises to show that it is morally permissible to lie to your children about Santa:

If you lie to your children about Santa Claus, then:

(1) They will have a lot of fun.
(2) When they figure out that Santa does not exist, they will learn valuable life lessons.
(3) You teach them the power of critical thinking.
(4) You do not really violate the "no lying" rule.

---

(5) It is morally permissible to lie to your children about Santa Claus.

Support for (1): Obviously it's fun to think about Santa and his reindeer, to leave cookies for Santa, to receive presents from him, etc.

Support for (2): Once a child who formerly believed in Santa realizes he doesn't exist, the child will learn that sometimes the world is profoundly different from the way we wish it was, that people lie to us, that people who lie to us sometimes do so out of love, that humans are a little crazy, etc.

Support for (3): Once a child gets to a certain age they should be able to figure out that the Santa story is highly implausible. The physics of the flying reindeer, of the fat guy getting down the chimney, and of visiting *every* child in the world in one night should be clues. The child who figures out on their own that Santa doesn't exist is likely to think, "I should have known this all along."

Support for (4): Children are not fully rational agents. They can't think that well yet. That's why we don't let them vote, for example. It's also why it is (sometimes, at least) permissible to lie to them. Lying to someone who is not a fully rational agent does not entail disrespect.

Con

Here is an argument for the moral impermissibility of lying to your children about Santa:

If you lie to your children about Santa Claus, then:

(1) They will feel betrayed and lose their trust in you.

(2) You will instill in them a materialistic attitude.

(3) They will develop unrealistic expectations and an unhealthy sense of entitlement.

(4) You act in a culturally insensitive manner.

---

(5) It is morally impermissible to lie to your children about Santa Claus.

Support for (1): Once a kid finds out that Santa doesn't exist, they will also discover that the people they trust more than anyone in the world made a concerted effort to lie to them for quite a while. That doesn't feel good. Moreover, when they realize that their trust was misplaced, they are likely to trust those people less in the future.

Support for (2): The main reason to like Santa is that he brings you stuff. Christmas isn't supposed to be about getting stuff. Nothing should be primarily about getting stuff.

Support for (3): Many young children, especially those from well-to-do families, get lots of presents from Santa. I have never known any parents to actually put coal in their children's stockings, even though I have known many parents with really poorly-behaved kids.

Children learn to *expect* gifts from a magical man. They think they *deserve* their presents, even though they clearly don't.

Support for (4): Obviously enough, Santa Claus is primarily a Christian thing. Don't you feel bad for the kids of different religions who don't get visited by Santa? Don't you think that kids who *do* get visited by Santa think that kids who don't are kind of weird?

VI. Self-Care

Is it ok to ...

27. Is it ok to gossip?

Clarification

Gossip takes the form of conversations about people's personal lives, usually involving rumors, hearsay, and unsubstantiated speculation. The person gossiped about is usually a mutual acquaintance of the gossipers.

Con

Given the very nature of gossip, it is very likely to involve spreading harmful falsehoods about people. It is wrong to knowingly harm others. Therefore, it is immoral to gossip.

Pro

Gossiping is a natural human activity that strengthens social bonds and fosters a feeling of community among gossipers. Gossiping can also serve to keep people informed about the wrongdoing of other community members. These positives outweigh any negatives associated with the activity and hence gossiping is morally permissible.

28. Is it ok to neglect your physical health?

Clarification

The question is whether it is morally permissible to eat unhealthy food, not exercise, drink too much alcohol, smoke and vape, or generally not care too much about living a "healthy lifestyle."

Pro

Of course it is permissible for you to neglect your body. It is your body, after all, and so you can do with it as you please. Even if it is not a good idea to let your body degrade very rapidly, it doesn't follow that there is anything immoral about doing so. It might not be a good idea to try to fix the kitchen faucet if you know nothing about plumbing, but the misguided DIYer doesn't act immorally. Similarly, it might not be a good idea to spend a week consuming nothing but ice cream, potato chips, and soda, but the misguided glutton doesn't act immorally. Again, if you're an adult, it is morally permissible for you to do with your own body as you please. This consideration is enough, all by itself, to show that it is permissible to let your body go.

Furthermore, it's not even obvious that it is a bad idea to let your health deteriorate, at least to some extent. A typical reason people give for living healthily is that they want to live longer. Fair enough, except that I fear people tend to think that living a long life is somehow *intrinsically* good. It's not. Perhaps it's better to live a relatively long life than a relatively short life, *assuming* that the long life is a good one. But there's nothing good about *just* living a long life. What's the point of living a long life if, in order to live a long life, you have to spend a lot of time doing things you don't want to do? Overeating can be fun. Drinking can be fun. Smoking can be fun. Exercise is a chore. Some people would rather die a few years earlier than give up the fun or bear the chore, and I don't see how you could argue that this preference is irrational. Plus, it's not like the healthy person's body isn't going to deteriorate eventually. On their death bed are they going to be happy that they refrained from a bunch of pleasures for many years so that they could add an extra two or five or ten years to their life?

In addition, even if you do place a lot of value on living a long life, you probably shouldn't try to live for *too* long. The reason is that even if you take really good care of your body, there is no guarantee that your mind will last as long. The worst-case scenario is that your mind goes long before your body does, and you spend years in a demented state. If you take really good care of your body, you increase the odds of this worst-case scenario occurring. Here's the ranking of the possible combinations, from best to worst:

(1) Your body and mind deteriorate at roughly the same time.

(2) Your body deteriorates long before your mind does.

(3) Your mind deteriorates long before your body does.

You really don't want (3) to happen, so it's probably not wise to take *really* good care of your body.

The default stance that a lot of people seem to take—that a healthy lifestyle and long life are somehow good in and of themselves—is a very questionable stance to take. Pretty clearly, if there is nothing all that great about a healthy lifestyle, then you can be under no moral obligation to live one. But it is worth repeating that the main reason why it is morally permissible to ignore your physical health is that you are allowed to do whatever you want with your own body. This reason is enough, all by itself, to prove the point.

Con

There are two different ways of understanding happiness. One way of understanding happiness can be used to show that it is probably in your best interest to live a healthy lifestyle. The other can be used to show that it is probably immoral not to live a healthy lifestyle.

The first conception of happiness is probably the one most people have. It says that happiness is a feeling. To be happy is just to have something like a joyous emotion. That's it. On this conception of happiness, happiness is incorrigible, meaning that if you think you're happy then you are. You can't be mistaken about your own happiness. Still, even if you think that you're happy doing what you do, you could be mistaken about whether you could be happi*er* doing something else. The gluttonous, slothful person might think that they are happy being gluttonous and slothful, and they'd be right. It doesn't follow, however, that they wouldn't be happier if they instead ate healthily and exercised. It is obvious that humans often have preferences that don't make them happy. The question is whether people feel happier living a healthy lifestyle or an unhealthy lifestyle. If all you know is one side—the unhealthy side—then you are not in a good position to determine whether the unhealthy lifestyle makes you happier than the healthy lifestyle. What we need, then, is some scientific evidence. And we have it. People who lead healthy lifestyles typically report higher rates of happiness than those who lead unhealthy lifestyles. Look it up. This strongly suggests that for selfish reasons you shouldn't let your body go.

So far, though, we haven't gotten to the moral issue of whether it is permissible to ignore your physical health. Maybe it's in your own interest not to, but that is not enough to show that you are obligated not to. In order to show *that*, we need to make use of a second conception of happiness. On this conception, happiness is corrigible, meaning that you can think that you're happy and be wrong. How is this possible? Answer: On the second conception of happiness, happiness is not primarily a feeling. Rather, happiness involves living a *good* life. Living a good life involves living as a human *should*. Living as a human should involves trying to live the best kind of human life that can be lived. The best kind of human life is determined by the kinds of creatures we are. On this conception of happiness, human lives have a purpose and that purpose is to try to lead an ideal human life. It is pretty clear that you can *think* you're coming close to leading an ideal human life and be mistaken. Furthermore, on this conception of happiness, you have a *moral* obligation to be happy. People who aren't happy are, in a very real sense, bad people. It is immoral to be a bad person, and therefore you have a moral obligation to be happy.

Consider a tool that doesn't work the way it's supposed to. For example, I have a cell phone that will not hold a charge for more than a few minutes. The battery is shot. The result is that my phone is a bad phone. Why? Because it doesn't do what cell phones are supposed to do. In fact, it's so bad at doing what it's supposed to do, that it becomes tempting to say that it no longer counts as a cell phone at all. If I tell you I have a cell phone, one of the things you will quite reasonably think is that you can call or text me when I'm out and about, as I walk down the street, for example. So if I say "I have a cell phone, but you can only call or text me when I'm home," it would be reasonable for you to respond with, "If you don't have a phone that works outside your house, then you don't have a cell phone."

Now, take this same line of reasoning and apply it to humans. An obvious case would be a "human" that never thinks. Such a thing functions so badly as a human that it's tempting to say that it doesn't count as a human. And that's basically right. But a human isn't *just* a thinking thing. It is a thing with a body that needs to function in a particular kind of way. If you *really* let your health deteriorate, then your unhealthy body will act as an obstacle to you partaking in other human activities that you must partake in to be a truly happy human. For example, a central human activity is entering into lots of different social arrangements with others. If you are too drunk or stinky to effectively enter into those social arrangements, then you are a bad human. It is immoral to be a bad human. Therefore, you do indeed have a moral obligation to take good care of your body. It is immoral to neglect your physical health.

29. Is it ok to be sexually promiscuous?

Clarification

To be sexually promiscuous is to be very sexually active, to have sex often and with multiple partners, and generally to adopt a casual attitude towards sex. Perhaps the best indicator of sexual promiscuity is engaging in sexual acts with someone when you are not in a "serious relationship" with that person.

Con

Here is an argument for the immorality of sexual promiscuity:

(1) Being sexually promiscuous increases the chances that you or your sexual partners will develop a sexually transmitted disease.
(2) Being sexually promiscuous increases the chances of unwanted pregnancy.
(3) Being sexually promiscuous diminishes the value of healthy long-term romantic relationships.
(4) Being sexually promiscuous involves using other people as tools for your own physical enjoyment.
(5) Being sexually promiscuous causes you to lose respect for yourself.

---

(6) It is morally impermissible to be sexually promiscuous.

Pro

To understand why it is morally permissible to be sexually promiscuous, consider two claims. The first is straightforward, and it's just that unless there is good reason to think that an action or pattern of behavior is morally wrong, you should think that it is morally permissible. In other words, the default position for any behavior should be that it is morally permissible. To take an obvious and trivial example, unless I have some reason to think that it is morally wrong for me to sleep on the couch instead of in my bed, I am probably safe assuming that it is ok for me to sleep on the couch. In any moral debate about the permissibility of an action, the burden of proof is on those who think the action is impermissible.

The second claim might be a bit trickier to fully appreciate, but it is more important. It is that arguments like the one given in the con essay can mislead you into thinking that good reasons have been given, when in fact they have not. The argument above offers several premises against promiscuity, and each of these reasons is supposed to make you doubt that sexual promiscuity is morally permissible. But note that if each premise is weak, then the fact that there are many (in this case five) premises doesn't make the argument a strong argument. A bunch of bad reasons is not somehow better than just one bad reason or no reasons at all. The argument above is a "shotgun argument." A shotgun emits a bunch of small metal bits at a target. This can be advantageous because even if most of the bits miss the target, a few will probably hit it, just because there are so many of them. This approach can often work in target shooting, but it often doesn't work too well in giving persuasive arguments. If none of the reasons are very good, you shouldn't be persuaded that the conclusion is true on the basis of such an argument. This is true whether there are three or five or twenty-five premises. Don't think, "Well, that person has a lot of reasons, so they're probably right." You have to look at each and every reason presented.

None of the premises in the argument above are good reasons for thinking that it is immoral to be sexually promiscuous. I will show how the first premise doesn't really do anything to get us to the conclusion, and I will leave it to you to determine why the other premises don't really constitute good reasons either. The first thing to note about the first premise—the one about STDs—is that *at best* it suggests that it is immoral to be sexually promiscuous *and* to not use protection. If the sexually promiscuous person insists on protected sex, then the first premise doesn't seem to apply. What this shows is that the first premise doesn't really have anything to do with sexual promiscuity. Again, at best it serves as a reason not to have unprotected sex.

Another potential problem with the first premise is that even if it is true that promiscuity increases the chances that someone will get an STD, it doesn't follow that the increase in risk is all that morally important. To see what I mean, let us suppose that if you engage in unprotected sex with multiple partners, your chances of getting any particular STD are five times higher than people who are not sexually promiscuous. I pulled that "five times" factor out of nowhere, but let's run with it. It seems *really high*. But even if your risk were to go up by a factor of five, is that enough to make the first premise a *moral* reason not to be sexually promiscuous? Well, let's turn to some actual data. By far the most common STD is chlamydia. According to the Centers for Disease Control and Prevention, in 2022 the rate of this relatively minor infection in the general population of the United States was 495 per 100,000 (compared to 389 / 100,000 for HIV and 17.7 / 100,000 for sexually transmitted syphilis). This means that about half of 1% of the population of the United States has chlamydia at a given time. Now, we're assuming that your risk factor goes up *five times* if you're sexually promiscuous. So what are the chances that you'll get chlamydia if you are sexually promiscuous? The answer is about 2,475 / 100,000, or about 2.5%. (It's actually a little bit lower than that, since the 495 / 100,000 number already includes sexually promiscuous people with chlamydia.) Now I am not suggesting that you shouldn't take notice of an increase in risk from half a percent to a little over two and a half percent. What I am suggesting is that this kind of increase is not likely to make for a very compelling moral case. People who drive or ride in cars have a much greater chance of being killed or seriously injured than people who don't, but presumably you wouldn't be convinced by any argument that tried to use this fact as a reason to show that driving and riding in cars is immoral.

The lesson is that the first premise in the argument in the con essay doesn't really serve as much of a reason for thinking that it is immoral to be sexually promiscuous. If, as I claim, all of the premises in the argument are like this, then the argument is a bad argument. The fact that it has *five* ultimately unconvincing premises is irrelevant. Add to this the assumption that the default position for any pattern of behavior should be that the behavior is morally permissible, and it sure looks like we should conclude that it is morally permissible to be sexually promiscuous. I hope I have convinced you that the first premise holds no weight. Please carefully consider the other premises. I think you will find that they are either false or irrelevant to the morality of promiscuity. If you do not find this to be the case—if you think that one or more premises is plausible and relevant to the main issue—then it might be a good exercise for you to try to make the case to others, either in discussion or in writing.

30. Is it ok to watch football?

Clarification

There has been a lot of controversy recently concerning the health risks to American football players who play in the National Football League (NFL). In particular, there is concern that many NFL players suffer repeated concussions and as a result develop a form of brain damage called chronic traumatic encephalopathy (CTE). One high profile case involved Junior Seau, a very good linebacker who played 20 seasons in the NFL. Seau died by suicide by shooting himself in the chest, perhaps because he wanted his brain to be examined after his death. It was indeed examined, and the findings strongly suggest that he suffered from CTE. Seau's case is not unique. Many former NFL players have been diagnosed with CTE after their deaths. People have called on the NFL to do more to protect players, and I think it safe to say that most advocates do not think the NFL has done enough. This might force us to ask whether it is permissible to watch NFL games. Let us assume that we're not asking about buying tickets to games or buying official merchandise, or doing anything else that might directly benefit the NFL. The question is whether it is ok even to watch NFL games on television.

Whatever you think about the morality of watching NFL games, the issue here need not be about football in particular. We might ask similar questions about watching boxing, mixed martial arts fighting, or ice hockey, for example. There are sport- and league-specific issues, of course. For example, one might also ask about the morality of watching NFL games, given the way the NFL has treated Colin Kaepernick and the way it has dealt with players who wish to kneel during the national anthem as a form of protest. These considerations are not obviously relevant to other leagues. But the current issue has to do with the morality of consuming violent entertainment that can seriously harm the performers. It is often useful to focus on a particular case, so let's stick with the NFL question.

Pro

While we all agree that it is unfortunate that so many NFL players have been harmed by playing professional football, it doesn't make much sense to suggest that merely watching an NFL game on television is morally wrong. By watching a game, I do not thereby *cause* players to get hurt. Or, at least, I don't cause them to get hurt in any way that makes me morally responsible.

Consider how the causal chain would look:

I watch NFL games on television → The NFL is able to continue what it's doing → Players continue to suffer serious, long-term injuries.

First, the first causal connection is highly questionable. This is especially obvious if I never buy tickets to any games and never buy NFL merchandise. *Maybe* if my television viewing habits were being monitored by the people who determine television ratings, then I would have some minor effect on the NFL's success, but I have never been one of the TV viewers they monitor.

Secondly, even if the first causal connection was a real one, it would be ridiculous to suggest that I am morally responsible for the end result. There are many causes of any event, and I am not morally responsible *every* time my actions play a very small causal role in a bad outcome. Consider this causal chain:

I sell a kitchen knife to Beatrice → Beatrice is able to continue her murderous ways → Beatrice stabs Jorge to death.

To say that *I* would be *at all* responsible for Jorge's murder defies all sense, even though I do play a (minor) role in the causal chain that leads to Jorge's death. Hence, the idea that my watching NFL games makes me responsible for NFL players getting hurt is wrong twice over. First, I'm not part of the cause of them getting hurt. Second, even if I were part of the cause, I would not be part of the cause in a way that would make me morally responsible. If I'm not morally responsible for the players' injuries, then it is very hard to see how I can be doing anything wrong.

If the causes of players developing brain damage are relevant to the moral aspect of the situation, then we need to focus on those causes that are more directly involved. One of those more imme-diate causes is the players' choice to play professional football. On the assumption that everyone knows the risks of an NFL career, the players have chosen, of their own free will, to take the risk of developing brain damage. This is not to say that players are to be *blamed* if they develop brain damage, but it does suggest that others, and in particular those of us who watch football on television, are in the moral clear. If the players *choose* to play a dangerous game in part because they think they will earn a lot of money doing so, then if they are harmed that is, to a large extent, *their* doing. I'm not suggesting that the NFL shouldn't do more to protect its players. What I *am* suggesting is that since those of us who watch football on TV are not forcing the players to play a dangerous game, it is inappropriate to blame us when they get hurt. If it is inappropriate to blame us for our actions, then there can't be anything wrong with our actions, and hence it is morally permissible to watch NFL games on television.

Con

Would you watch a public spectacle in which people are fed to vicious dogs? I hope not. Do you see that there is a problem with just watching such a thing, even if you can't say, exactly, what is wrong with it? Or consider another example. There are assholes who pay homeless people to fight and then post videos of the fights online because other assholes somehow find it enjoyable to watch vulnerable people hurt each other. Imagine an aficionado of so-called bum fights. Would you want such a person to look after young children? I hope you have reservations. Watching people get hurt, whatever its entertainment value, is wrong. This is exactly what you're doing when you watch NFL football—watching people get hurt. You know the players are getting hurt—and I don't mean merely that you're watching linemen who will have achy knees for the rest of their lives: you're watching people develop severe and debilitating *brain damage*. That's wrong for the same reason that it's wrong to watch people get fed to dogs.

One objection to my argument might be that football watchers do not watch football *in order to* watch people get hurt. They watch football in order to see exciting and amazing athletic competitions. That people are getting hurt is an unfortunate side effect of these competitions. Nobody watches football for the injuries. Therefore, the objection goes, watching football is nothing like watching people get fed to dogs or watching homeless people fight each other. In the latter two cases, the violence is the whole point, but that's not so with football.

A second objection involves something mentioned in the pro essay, namely that NFL players have chosen to try to make a career out of playing football even though they know the risks. Isn't that enough to show that football watchers are off the moral hook?

I think both objections can be dealt with if we consider another example. This one is from fiction, but it's no worse an example because of that. In both the TV show *Game of Thrones* and the book series *A Song of Ice and Fire* on which the show is based, the character Daenerys Targaryen takes her army to the city of Meereen. Meereen is a slave city, and a popular recreational activity there is to watch slaves fight each other to the death in the fighting pits. People who watch the slave fights do not watch primarily to see people being killed. The spectators appreciate the great skill of the combatants, many of whom train for years and are indeed great athletes as well as great fighters. But isn't there still something wrong with watching slaves fight to the death? Yes. So much for the first objection above. The spectators at the fighting pits don't watch to see death. They watch to appreciate great skill. Football watchers don't watch to see people get brain damaged. They watch to appreciate great skill. Nonetheless, the spectators at the fighting pits act immorally. This shows that the first objection fails.

Still, as long as the fighting pit combatants are slaves, maybe the second objection stands. The slaves have no choice but to fight if that's what their masters command. This is not true of NFL players. There is, however, a twist to the story. Daenerys conquers Meereen and frees all slaves. She also closes the fighting pits, but later, under pressure from the former ruling class and even some former slaves, she reluctantly reopens them. Afterwards, people are allowed to *volunteer* to fight to the death in the pits, and many do. Here's the point: If it was wrong for spectators to enjoy fights to the death when the combatants were slaves, then it is wrong when they enjoy fights to the death between those who have chosen to fight. Why would you think otherwise? It's the to-the-death part that makes it wrong to watch the fights, not the choice or lack thereof of the fighters. Similarly, it's the developing-brain-damage part that makes it wrong to watch football, not the choice or lack thereof of the players.

VII. Taboos

Is it ok to ...

31. Is it ok to tell off-color jokes?

Clarification

An off-color joke is a joke that is likely to be viewed as vulgar, rude, insensitive, offensive, or even bigoted. I'm afraid we need a couple of examples, so brace yourself. In 2015 Germanwings Flight 9525 crashed, killing all 150 people on board. The crash was caused by the mentally ill co-pilot who locked the pilot out of the cabin when he took a bathroom break. The co-pilot intentionally put the plane into a steep dive and it crashed in the French Alps. Later, Timothy Bell, a former election advisor to Margaret Thatcher, told a knock-knock joke live on the BBC: "Knock-knock. Who's there? The pilot." Here's another (this one is worse) that I heard Sarah Silverman tell. A child molester and a little boy are walking deeper and deeper into a wooded area. It's literally a dark and stormy night. The boy turns to the child molester and says, "I'm scared." The child molester responds, "You're scared?! I have to walk out of here alone!" Our question is whether it is morally permissible to tell such jokes when they are likely to offend someone in your audience.

Pro

The obvious point to make in favor of the moral permissibility of telling off-color jokes is that telling such jokes does no harm. Very importantly, offending someone is very different than harming them, and it is very difficult to see how a joke can *harm*. And if no harm is done, then the burden is on those who think telling off-color jokes is morally wrong.

But the case for telling off-color jokes goes deeper than the no-harm point. Humor is, by its very nature, something that challenges taboos. As Mark Twain said, "The funniest things are the forbidden." It is very difficult to tell a funny joke without ruffling a few feathers. Or, to put the same point a different way, good, clean, family-appropriate jokes almost always suck. Think of the jokes young children tell or the "jokes" you might find in newspaper comics. ("Why shouldn't you use a broken pencil? Because it's pointless.") They don't even make you laugh a little on the inside.

Comedy has to be at least a little bit edgy in order to be comedy, i.e., in order to be funny. This is why there is some truth to the claim that people who are constantly offended by this or that lack a sense of humor. Comedians and successful joke tellers know that a good way to get people to laugh at a joke is to push boundaries. No doubt, sometimes they push the boundaries too far and stray into the realm where their jokes aren't edgy but rather tasteless. All this shows, though, is that writing (and telling) a funny joke is difficult. Whenever you try to gain some benefit, there's an accompanying risk. Tastelessness and offensiveness are the risks associated with the benefits of humor. If we are to have funny jokes, then we have to pay the cost. I, for one, think the benefit is worth the cost, and I trust you agree. The reason it's ok to tell off-color jokes is that it's ok to tell jokes. You can't do the latter without doing the former, unless you want all your jokes to be lame.

Con

There is a common and tempting view of humans, according to which we have personalities and character traits and they cause us to behave in particular ways. For example, some people are just shy. That is one of their character traits. Their shyness in turn causes them to not speak up in class, to avoid certain kinds of social gatherings, etc. This picture is perhaps accurate up to a point, but it leaves out something very important. What it leaves out is that your behavior can have a causal impact on your personality and character traits. We tend to think there is a one-way causal street:

character traits → behavior

But, as a matter of psychological fact, the street is two-way:

character traits ↔ behavior

The shy person who goes out of their way to speak up in class or to go to a party where there will be a lot of people they don't know might become less shy.

Furthermore, just as your character traits might cause you to do either moral or immoral things, your behavior can cause you to have good or bad character traits. And now we're in a position to see what is wrong with telling off-color jokes. Telling such jokes can damage you as a person; telling the jokes might worsen your character traits. In particular, you might become less empathetic and less caring of your fellow humans. A characteristic of most off-color jokes is that they involve a kind of callousness toward a person or group of people. This callousness can rub off on the joke teller and make them less sensitive to other people's suffering, other people's desires, the struggles that other people face, etc.

Note that we're not talking about the phenomenon of passive desensitization. We're not talking about the kind of desensitization that might occur when you *listen* to an off-color joke or the kind of desensitization that might occur when you *watch* violence in movies and television. Actually *doing* violence is likely to harm your character worse than merely watching violence. Similarly, *telling* off-color jokes is likely to harm your character worse than merely *hearing* them.

The lesson is that if you tell off-color jokes you run a huge risk, and it's not just the risk of offending others. It's the risk of damaging yourself as a person. The damage is not so immediate or obvious as the damage done to your body if you're hit in the head with a two-by-four, but that is to be expected. Psychological damage can be subtle and hard to detect. So if you're thinking anything like, "Telling off-color jokes just isn't going to make me any worse a person," I urge you to question this assumption. If it's hard to know when you're being psychologically and morally damaged, you shouldn't be so sure that telling off-color jokes won't damage your character. It can never be morally permissible to damage your character. Telling off-color jokes increases the risk that you will damage your character, and that is why it is wrong to tell off-color jokes, no matter who your audience is.

It is also worth mentioning that despite what is claimed in the pro essay, there is a lot of genuinely funny stuff that doesn't involve off-color jokes. For one thing, humor can be "edgy" without being callous. Second, humor doesn't have to be edgy in order to be funny. There are many examples. We don't have to give up on humor if we give up on off-color jokes. Even when they're funny, telling off-color jokes is not worth the risk.

32. Is it ok to judge people on the basis of their appearance?

Clarification

The question is not whether we do in fact judge people based on the way they look. Of course we often do. However, there is an important distinction between how we actually behave and how we ought to behave. The word "judge" in the question is to be understood in the usual way. To judge is to make a determination of the value of someone or something. Note that we can judge people or things to be good or bad or neutral. The word "appearance" should also be taken pretty literally. We're talking about the way people *look* to us. (We could also ask whether it is ok to judge people on the basis of their accents or dialects, but that's an issue for another time.)

Imagine that you're walking down the street and you see a group of people walking toward you. For whatever reason, you don't like the looks of them, so you cross the street in order to avoid coming in close proximity to them. It is obvious to everyone, including the members of the group, that you crossed the street to avoid them. Is your action morally permissible?

Con

(1) If it is morally permissible to judge people on the basis of their appearance, then it is morally permissible to judge people on the basis of their race or gender.

(2) It is not morally permissible to judge people on the basis of their race or gender.

(3) It is not morally permissible to judge people on the basis of their appearance.

Pro

Imagine a man, dressed head to toe in black, wearing a ski mask, and carrying a long knife with some sort of red liquid dripping from it. Call this man The Man in Black.

(1) If it is not morally permissible to judge people on the basis of their appearance, then it is not morally permissible to judge The Man in Black on the basis of his appearance.
(2) It is morally permissible to judge The Man in Black on the basis of his appearance.

---

(3) It is morally permissible to judge people on the basis of their appearance.

Option 3—It depends.

(1) If it is always morally permissible to judge people on the basis of their appearance, then it is morally permissible to judge people on the basis of their race or gender.
(2) If it is never permissible to judge people on the basis of their appearance, then it is morally impermissible to judge The Man in Black on the basis of his appearance.
(3) It is not morally permissible to judge people on the basis of their race or gender.
(4) It is morally permissible to judge The Man in Black on the basis of his appearance.

---

(5) Sometimes it is morally permissible to judge people on the basis of their appearance, and sometimes it is not.

Question: When is it ok to judge on the basis of appearance and when is it not?
Answer: I don't know. That's a hard question, but both the con and pro sides are obviously wrong about the whole issue.

33. Is it ok to speak ill of the dead?

Clarification

There seems to be a social norm that we shouldn't say bad things about dead people because they are dead. The question is whether it is morally permissible to violate that norm.

Pro

It is morally permissible to speak ill of the dead for the same reason that it is morally permissible to speak ill of the living. People don't somehow magically obtain a special status when they die. Nobody deserves reverence because they no longer exist. How does dying make them deserve better than what they deserved when they were alive? If anything, the dead are *less* deserving because they can't feel pleasure or pain, they can't reason, they don't care about anything, etc.

Obviously it is sometimes permissible to criticize others. There are cases when you shouldn't but that is beside the point. If it is *ever* morally permissible to criticize the living, then it is morally permissible to criticize the dead. Again, you are probably on safer moral ground criticizing the dead because dead people will never find out about your negative comments.

Con

Maybe in a perfect world all social norms, conventions, and institutions would be completely rational in every conceivable way. I say "maybe" and that's a big "maybe." It might not be too pleasant for humans to live in a perfectly rational world. But let us assume that a perfect world for humans is a perfectly rational world in which all of our norms, conventions, and institutions make perfect sense. This assumption doesn't really help us to figure out how we should live in the *actual* world, with all of its irrationality. The point is this: From the fact that a social prohibition on saying pejorative things about a dead person is irrational, it doesn't follow that it's morally permissible to just ignore the prohibition.

There are all sorts of social rules that are not legal rules and that don't make a lot of sense. Why are you not supposed to put your elbows on the table when dining? Why is it expected that a man will wear a tie in certain formal situations? Why is it considered rude to ask someone you've just met how old they are or how much they paid for their house? It's not clear that these social rules serve any rational purpose, and there are many examples of such norms. But if you were to go around breaking all of these rules, not only would you be *considered* a jerk, you would *be* a jerk.

Like laws, sometimes social norms effectively serve a purpose and sometimes they don't. Now, whether it is ok to break a pointless law is a difficult question. But when we're talking about harmless social norms, it is wrong to knowingly violate them unless you have other, very good moral reasons to do so. And this is true regardless of whether they effectively serve a purpose. Social norms are the glue that holds society together. When you ignore a social norm because you don't think it makes any sense, you're in effect saying to other people that you don't care too much about the cooperation that is necessary for a society to exist in the first place. It is one thing to merely flout convention by, say, dressing in an unusual manner. But when others expect you to act in a particular way *and* you know that they would be displeased if you were to act contrary to their expectations, it is generally not ok for you to do so.

Note that the problem with violating social norms is not that some horrible situation will immediately follow. Rather, the problem has to do with what you're communicating to your fellow humans when you violate a norm. Again, the norm violator in effect says, "Screw you guys, I'm going home," simply because they don't like the norms. The social norm violator is also a lot like the jerk who agrees to play a board game with others but then flips the table over because they start to lose and doesn't like the rules of the game. Just as the rules of a board game might be improved upon, social norms might also be made more rational. And just as it's wrong for the game player to flip over the table, it's wrong for a member of society to violate harmless social norms. What follows is that if you live in a society that prohibits speaking ill of the dead, it is morally wrong for you to speak ill of the dead.

34. Is it ok to celebrate someone's death?

Clarification

The question is whether it is morally permissible to *show* happiness because someone has died. (The question is not about how you should *feel*.) Let us assume that we are not talking about showing happiness in the presence of those who loved the deceased. Presumably, the individual who feels happy because of someone's death either hates the deceased or thinks the world will somehow be a better place because the dead person is no longer around. People certainly celebrate the deaths of brutal dictators. Sometimes people celebrate when a convicted murderer is put to death by the state. I know someone who celebrated Ronald Reagan's death. But the dead person doesn't have to be (in)famous or very influential. Perhaps you wouldn't be able to help feeling a little bit happy if your inconsiderate neighbor, your racist uncle, or that guy who just cut you off in traffic were to drop dead. But would it be ok for you to let others know that you're happy about it?

Pro

(1) If a good event occurs, then it is appropriate to celebrate that event.

(2) Sometimes a person's death is a good event.

(3) Sometimes it is appropriate to celebrate a person's death.

Con

(1) If a not-good event occurs, then it is not appropriate to celebrate that event.

(2) A person's death is never a good event.

(3) It is never appropriate to celebrate a person's death.

35. Is it ok to reveal spoilers?

Clarification

A spoiler is a piece of information about the plot of a piece of fiction that is inadvertently consumed by a person who doesn't want to consume it, because they do not want to know about important plot features of a story they have not yet read or watched, but which they plan to read or watch. If you haven't read *A Dance with Dragons* or watched season five of *A Game of Thrones*, but plan to do so, then [SPOILER ALERT] I would "spoil" it for you by telling you that Jon Snow is stabbed to death by some members of the Night's Watch at the very end of the book/season. Our question is whether it is morally permissible to spoil. You spoil when you do *not* take great care to avoid revealing plot twists to people who don't want to know them. If, despite your best efforts, you accidentally spoil a plot for someone, then you cannot be blamed for that; but can you be blamed if you spoil the plot for someone because either you just didn't think too much about spoiling or because you didn't mind spoiling?

Con

It is morally impermissible to reveal spoilers, and this can be shown pretty easily: When you reveal a spoiler, you *spoil* a story for other people. You needlessly decrease their enjoyment. It is morally wrong to needlessly decrease good stuff in the world, and enjoyment of fiction is part of the good stuff.

Pro

There are two main reasons why it is morally permissible to reveal spoilers. First, to say that it is always wrong to reveal spoilers is to put too much of a moral burden on people. If you have a moral principle that is so stringent that nobody can ever live up to it, then the problem might be with your principle, not the people who fail to live up to it. Am I really not supposed to talk about the most recent episode of a television show with my friend on the bus, because there *might* be another passenger who *might* hear us and who plans on watching the episode later? That seems way too strict. Do I really have to be careful not to spoil plots even of stories that have been around for a long time? I have never seen the movie *The Village*. A friend of mine just recently told me how it ends without first asking whether I wanted to know. I was not angry. First, I think movies by M. Night Shyamalan tend to suck, but more importantly, even if I really wanted to watch *The Village* and didn't want to know how it ends, it is surely relevant that the movie was released in 2004. It would be unreasonable to expect my friend not to reveal the plot twist of a movie that old. If someone hasn't watched a movie that old, then surely all bets are off when it comes to spoiling it for them. Otherwise, it would be hard for any of us to have even casual conversations about fiction, which is itself an enjoyable activity. It seems that the do-not-spoil rule is too strict, and hence cannot be a moral rule.

The second reason why it is morally permissible to reveal spoilers is that doing so doesn't really have much of an impact on people's enjoyment of works of fiction. Suppose I tell you that I'm about to show you a painting that I really like and then say, "Spoiler alert: It's a landscape." Do you really think that the "spoiler" here is going to adversely affect your enjoyment of the painting? No. Now, a painting is not a book or a movie, but the example serves to show that more often than not, what is enjoyable about art—whether it is fiction or not—is not the information it conveys, but rather *how* that information is conveyed. A no-talent hack can represent some haystacks on canvas, but Monet does it in a really cool way, and that's why people tend to think he was a great painter.

Now consider an example concerning a piece of fiction. The example works best if you have never seen the 1941 movie *Citizen Kane*.

[SPOILER ALERT] "Rosebud" is the name on the sled Kane had when he was a boy.

If you haven't ever seen the movie, did I just ruin it for you? Did I just spoil what is considered by many to be the best film ever made? I think not. If you are completely unfamiliar with the movie, then if anything, my "spoiler" should intrigue you and make you *more* eager to watch it, not less. If I'm right (and I am), then the argument against revealing spoilers relies on a very questionable premise, namely that spoilers significantly and adversely affect people's enjoyment of fiction. People might *think* that their enjoyment will be diminished if they encounter a spoiler, but what people think their experiences will be like and what they are actually like are often two very different things. Furthermore, because (a) it is difficult to constantly go out of your way to avoid revealing spoilers and (b) it is enjoyable to discuss fiction with others even if that means you occasionally reveal spoilers, the bad of revealing spoilers does not outweigh the good. It follows that revealing spoilers is not morally wrong.

VIII. Identity Issues

Is it ok to ...

36. Is it ok to proselytize?

Clarification

In this context, to proselytize is to go out of your way to talk to people about your religion, to try to convince them that your religion is true, helpful, meaningful, or in some way good, and even to try to convert people to your religion. We will consider the would-be Christian or Muslim proselytizer, just to have a couple of examples, but the same question can be asked for other religions. Our would-be proselytizer could be Hindu, Jewish, or Sikh, for example. Fill in the blank with whichever religion you like (unless the religion forbids or discourages its followers from proselytizing). We might even ask whether it is morally permissible for an atheist to try to convince other people that they should give up their religion. Note that we're not talking about merely discussing your religion (or atheism) with others or answering questions about your religion. We're talking about cases where you might try to get others to accept your religion when they have shown no initial interest. Think of Jehovah's Witnesses knocking on your door.

Pro

(A1) If it is morally permissible to be a Christian or a Muslim, then it is morally permissible to proselytize in the name of Christianity or Islam.
(A2) It is morally permissible to be a Christian or a Muslim.

(A3) It is morally permissible to proselytize in the name of Christianity or Islam.

Support for (A1):

(B1) If it is morally permissible to be a Christian or a Muslim, then it is morally permissible to do what Christianity or Islam commands.

(B2) Christianity commands proselytizing in the name of Christianity.

(B3) Islam commands proselytizing in the name of Islam.

(B4) If it is morally permissible to be a Christian or a Muslim, then it is morally permissible to proselytize in the name of Christianity or Islam.

Support for (B2):
from the Christian Bible (New American Standard translation), Matthew 28:19–20:

> "Go therefore and make disciples of all the nations, baptizing them in the name of the Father and the Son and the Holy Spirit, teaching them to observe all that I have commanded you; and lo, I am with you always, even to the end of the age."

Support for (B3):
from the Qur'an (Saheeh International translation), An-Nahl 16:125:

> "Invite to the way of your Lord with wisdom and good instruc-tion, and argue with them in a way that is best. Indeed, your Lord is most knowing of who has strayed from His way, and He is most knowing of who is [rightly] guided."

Con

(C1) It is morally permissible to proselytize in the name of Christianity or Islam only if there are good reasons for believing that Christianity or Islam is true.

(C2) There are no good reasons for believing that Christianity or Islam is true.

(C3) It is not morally permissible to proselytize in the name of Christianity or Islam.

Support for (C1):

(D1) If it is morally permissible to proselytize in the name of Christianity or Islam and there are no good reasons for believing that Christianity or Islam is true, then it is morally permissible to try to brainwash people.

(D2) It is not morally permissible to try to brainwash people.

(D3) It is morally permissible to proselytize in the name of Christianity or Islam only if there are good reasons for believing that Christianity or Islam is true.

Support for (C2):

(E1) If there are good reasons for believing that Christianity or Islam is true, then there is either compelling scientific evidence for their truth or there are good arguments for their truth.

(E2) There is no compelling scientific evidence for the truth of either Christianity or Islam.

(E3) There are no good arguments for the truth of either Christianity or Islam.

(E4) There are no good reasons for believing that Christianity or Islam is true.

37. Is it ok to be patriotic?

Clarification

I take it that we all have some idea of what patriotic attitudes and behaviors are. Is it morally permissible to have these attitudes, and even more importantly, is it morally permissible to speak and act patriotically?

Con

This is easy. Patriotism is pretty much an all-around bad phenomenon. First, it doesn't make much sense in the first place to behave patriotically. Second, patriotism is irritating to other people. Third, patriotism is responsible for some of the worst evils ever perpetrated.

Patriotism doesn't make a lot of sense in that it involves being proud of one's nationality. Nobody would say they are a patriotic American but also ashamed to be American, and it seems pride is the essence of patriotism. But pride in what, exactly? The vast majority of people live in and are citizens of the country they were born in. Hence, for most people, to be proud of being American or Canadian or Chinese or Russian or whatever is to be proud of being born in a particular place at a particular point in time. Obviously, that's nothing to be proud of, since where and when you're born is a matter of dumb luck. Being proud to be an American is like being proud to be right-handed.

Here's the test for whether it makes sense to be proud of something: Could you reasonably expect people to congratulate you for it? If the answer is no, then it's hard to understand why anyone would feel pride about it. Did you earn a degree? Congratulations. You should be proud of your accomplishment. Did you get married? Congratulations. Be proud of the marital bliss you've managed to find. But nobody is ever going to say, "You were born Belgian?! Way to go!" National origin fails the congratulation test, and so national pride doesn't make a lot of sense.

Furthermore, when you go out of your way to make patriotic displays, you needlessly annoy other people. Note to Americans:

The whole rest of the world rolls its eyes when the chant "USA! USA!" is heard at international sporting competitions. Note to Canadians: Everyone else thinks that the maple leaf you have sewn on your backpack is incredibly obnoxious. Note to the Chinese: People of other countries know that Chinese culture is very old and are painfully aware that you think China will one day regain its rightful place as the most powerful and most important country in the world. They either don't care or fear China's rise. I could continue with this public service to the people of the world, but you get the point.

Still, maybe the fact that patriotism is irritating isn't enough to show that it's all that bad. This brings me to my third point. It is the strongest and easiest of the three to make and it's that people do *awful* things in the name of patriotism and the nationalism that accompanies it. As evidence I ask you to consider the entire history of the nation-state. Pay particular attention to the twentieth century and especially two little events called World War I and World War II. They are particularly striking examples of what patriotism and nationalism can do, but there are many, many other examples. Patriotism and nationalism play such a massive role in humans killing each other that when religion is criticized for being a death machine, some religious people use the "defense" that at least religion hasn't been responsible for as many needless deaths as secular nation-states have been. It would be bad enough if patriotism were responsible for "just" millions and millions of needless deaths, but it is also at least partially responsible for displacing huge numbers of people, for cultural genocides, and for destroying a lot of really cool stuff. If there is widespread violation of fundamental human rights going on, there's sure to be a group of patriots nearby.

Pro

Nobody can seriously question that patriotism and nationalism have a long history of making people behave very badly. It does not follow, however, that you are morally prohibited from behaving patriotically. Like religion, patriotism can play an important role in a good human life. One of the reasons why is that humans, being social creatures, have a natural tendency to want to belong to a group. Patriotism is an example of this tendency that is specific to the group of people with whom you share a country.

It seems that, in addition to notions of fairness, liberty, care, respect, and purity, *loyalty* is one of the bases for our moral thought. Loyalty involves something like standing up for your side. So, in order to be loyal, you have to know which side is yours. Humans quite naturally and usually fairly easily make the distinction between those who are in their in-group (their "side") and those who are in their out-group (the people not on their side). This is morally relevant: we think standing up for your in-group is loyalty and is good, while standing with the out-group is betrayal and is bad. (This is a plausible and potentially very explanatorily powerful theory of how and why humans think about ethics.)

Now, it would be fallacious to argue that because patriotism is natural it's also morally permissible. But because we have the tendency to think in terms of our in-group, and because patriotism is one example of this tendency, two points in favor of patriotism are fairly easy to make. First, to tell people that they shouldn't have patriotic attitudes or behave patriotically might be to tell people not to do something they can't help but do, given that patriotism has an innate basis. Since "ought" implies "can"—since it is at least very weird to tell people that they shouldn't do something they can't possibly help but do—then if we feel patriotic because of an innate disposition, it is at least very weird for anyone to say that we shouldn't feel patriotic. Patriotism is, after all, a feeling more than anything else. You don't logically deduce your patriotism or *decide* to be patriotic on the basis of scientific or observational evidence. It is a feeling—and I, for one, have never understood any claim to the effect that one shouldn't *feel* a certain way. If I feel bad, it might make sense for you to try to cheer me up, but it doesn't make much sense for you to say that I should not feel bad. Look, if I feel bad I feel bad; it's not like I'm *trying* to feel bad. I haven't *decided* to feel bad. I just do feel bad. Feelings are like that. Patriotism is primarily a feeling, and so telling patriotic people that they shouldn't feel patriotic is not a very helpful thing to say.

Second, even if we could rid ourselves of patriotism, it's not clear that we should, assuming that it is at least partially due to an innate module in our brains. I think that happy humans are those that feel a sense of belonging with other humans. It is no accident that our tendency to make in-group/out-group distinctions is innate. Belonging to a group and "siding" with it is a central part of a rich social life, and a rich social life is more likely to be a happy life. It's hard to just *be* social in the sense of having social connections that one finds important. You're not social in the relevant sense just by acting friendly toward strangers or by having 327 Facebook "friends." To have meaningful social connections, we need to find common ground with others. Patriotism is partly the effect of us finding common ground with other people and it is partly the cause of our ability to find common ground with our fellow citizens. Feeling patriotic and behaving patriotically is not the only way of achieving a sense of belonging with others, but it is a significant one.

You can also feel a sense of belonging by cheering for a particular sports team. Any die-hard fan knows that part of the irresistibility of cheering for your team is that you celebrate with your co-fans when your team wins and commiserate with them when your team loses. Without that fellow feeling, nobody would have any reason to be a Toronto Maple Leafs fan, for example. All Toronto hockey fans *have* is the commiseration (and perhaps unrealistic hope). The point is that if something as trivial as the performance of your favored sports team can give you a sense of belonging, if something so very unimportant can provide you with happy-making social connections, then surely something genuinely important, such as the well-being of your country and society, can do so even better. Most people would not want to rid themselves of their patriotism even if they could, and for good reason.

38. Is it ok to appropriate another culture?

Clarification

The question is most pressing for those who are in a cultural majority or members of a culturally dominant group who might want to adopt aspects of a minority culture. For example, in the United States, most white non-immigrant people are members of the culturally dominant group. Is it ok for white Americans, in their daily lives, to appropriate aspects of African American culture, Native American culture, Hindu culture, etc.? Or are these examples of cultural *mis*appropriation?

Con

Cultural appropriation is disrespectful. That's why it's wrong. It is especially disrespectful when the aspect being appropriated is considered to be of major importance to the culture in question. I don't mean to pick on white Westerners who do yoga or even to suggest that white people doing yoga always constitutes cultural appropriation, but the watered-down unintentional parody of real yoga some Westerners do is an illustration of this disrespect, and shows the moral impermissibility of cultural appropriation in general.

All persons deserve respect. You must always consider the goals and values of rational agents when you act. When you blithely appropriate others' cultures, you do not consider the goals and values of the members of those cultures.

It is important to note two things about disrespect. First, to disrespect someone is not merely to offend them or "hurt their feelings." It is more serious than that. You might be offended by my opinion of your religious beliefs, for example, but as long as I acknowledge your ability to think critically about your religious beliefs, I am not disrespecting you when I offer my opinion.

Second, you can disrespect someone without intending to do so. (You can also accidentally offend someone, but remember that we are not talking about mere offense.) When you disrespect someone, it is no defense to say, "But I didn't *mean* to" or "I meant no harm." When people begin a criticism with "No disrespect, but ..." they do not get a magical moral free ride. If what follows this phrase is in fact disrespectful, then the little "no disrespect" preamble does nothing. The whole problem with disrespecting others is that it is a failure to recognize their interests. Clearly, you can fail to recognize someone's interests without *intending* to do wrong, but you have still done wrong. Imagine a person walking down a busy corridor with their head down, looking at their phone. Suppose they bump into someone. That's rude. It doesn't really matter that they didn't *mean* to bump into other people. The reason they are rude is that they give no thought to the people they share the world with. Their rudeness can be *defined* as their lack of respect for others. Similarly, those who appropriate others' cultures usually don't give much thought to the people whose culture they're appropriating. That's incredibly disrespectful, and it's wrong to act disrespectfully.

Pro

There are two reasons why there is nothing wrong with cultural appropriation.

Reason 1: If you live in the West, and certainly if you live in North America, then you live in a culture that places great importance on personal freedom. Our laws and indeed pretty much all of our society are based on the notion that individuals get to choose for themselves how to live their lives. I happen to think that this foundational principle is a good one. If you agree, then you should also agree that whenever there is a question about the morality of an individual's actions, we should err on the side of saying that their actions are morally permissible. (We should also err on the side of saying that their actions are lawful, but I'm not making a legal claim. I'm making a stronger, ethical claim.) So, even if, *on some occasions*, there might be something a little bit morally icky when somebody appropriates from another culture, we have to say that that individual's right to act as they please trumps the little bit of ickiness. In other words, because personal freedom is the very foundation on which our society is based, it is more important than the considerations brought up in the con essay. Sometimes individuals choose to exercise their freedom by appropriating others' cultures. Given our commitments to individual freedom, we should adopt the view that it is morally permissible for individuals to appropriate cultures.

Reason 2: Often when people are wrong about an ethical issue, it's not because they've reasoned poorly about ethics itself, but rather because they're mistaken about some non-ethical fact. For example, consider a well-educated European man living in the sixteenth century. He is almost certainly a sexist. We can imagine that he is kind-hearted and that he wants to behave ethically. Yet he behaves unethically toward women. Why? Well, it seems he is just wrong about a non-ethical fact. He thinks that women on the whole are not as smart or capable as men. This false claim is not obviously an *ethical* claim. I don't take myself to be stating anything about ethics when I say that cats can't do calculus. I just think that it is a non-ethical fact that cats can't do calculus. Our sixteenth-century sexist just thinks that it is a non-ethical fact that women don't have what it takes to contribute to society in the same way men do. My cat-belief doesn't seem to be about ethics and it is true. The sexist's women-belief doesn't seem to be about ethics and it is false. Furthermore, it is this false belief that causes him to behave in a way that we recognize to be immoral.

I suggest that something similar is going on with those who think that cultural appropriation is immoral. It's not that they're making a mistake about which moral principles are true; they're right to emphasize the importance of respect, for example. No, their real mistake concerns the relevant non-ethical facts and specifically the fact that, to a very large extent, any culture just *is* a collection of cultural appropriations. Any culture just *is* a lot of stuff from other cultures, whether those other cultures exist today or long ago. American culture is a good example. It has appropriated *a lot* from eighteenth-century English culture (which in turn took a lot from other cultures). It has taken a lot from various cultures of Continental Europe, Africa, from Native American cultures, French-Canadian culture, its own past culture, and others. Take all of these appropriations away, and what would be left of American culture? Nothing. Language is obviously a huge aspect of culture. What languages would Americans speak without cultural appropriation? Or consider other aspects of culture. Without appropriation, what foods would Americans eat?

What sports would they play? What would their music sound like? Would they put on plays or produce movies? To try to answer these questions one has to try to imagine the impossible: an American culture that never borrowed this or that from other, already existing cultures. Furthermore, although the American case makes for a striking example, it is not unique. *All* cultures have done *a lot* of borrowing from others, as any historian or geographer can tell you.

The main point is that to have a problem with cultural appropriation is to have a problem with culture itself. As far as I know, nobody objects to the very notion of culture, so nobody should object to cultural appropriation either. The critics of cultural appropriation seem to miss a non-ethical fact: the fact that culture just is cultural appropriation from the very start. Their mistake makes them reach the wrong moral verdict.

39. Is it ok to make use of stereotypes about races, ethnicities, genders, etc. when those stereotypes are seemingly positive?

Clarification

The use of stereotypes involves the attribution of traits to identifiable groups of people. It is taken for granted that making negative generalizations about a group of people is morally wrong. The question has to do with the attribution of traits that are widely regarded as positive or traits that are widely regarded as neither particularly good nor bad. For example, is it ok to make use of the stereotype that says people of East Asian descent are good at math?

Pro

It is morally ok to use a stereotype when it involves the attribution of a trait that the user of the stereotype thinks is a good trait for people to have or when the user thinks the trait is neither good nor bad.

The reason it is morally permissible to use positive or neutral stereotypes is that when you do so, you do not cause any harm. Here is the argument:

(1) The use of a stereotype is morally permissible if:
(a) the stereotype is true when understood as a loose generalization
and
(b) the use of the stereotype does not cause anyone any harm.

(2) Some positive stereotypes are true when understood as loose generalizations and some of the same positive stereotypes do not cause anyone any harm.

---

(3) The use of some positive stereotypes is morally permissible.

Consider the first premise first. The most important part of that premise is clause (b). The Harm Principle simply says that if an action doesn't cause either the actor or anyone else any harm, then the action is not morally wrong. I will not defend the Harm Principle thoroughly here. Instead I will just ask you to consider whether you think it is correct. If you deny the Harm Principle, then you think there are actions that don't cause any harm to anyone at all (even in the long term) and yet those actions are morally wrong. I, for one, have a hard time imagining such an action. Clause (a) is included in the first premise simply because positive but false stereotypes can do harm indirectly, since they might make us act on the basis of faulty information and hence might make us do something that does cause harm, even when we do not intend to.

The second premise is true because, first, there are loose generalizations about people that are true. It is true that *as a group* American students of East Asian descent score better on standardized math tests and in mathematics courses than American students of Western European descent. Note that when someone says something like "Asians are good at math," they do not mean *every* person of Asian descent is better at math than *every* person of European descent. This is the sense in which stereotypes are properly understood as loose generalizations. Note too that someone who says, "Asians are good at math" is not committed to the idea that there is something inherent in being Asian that makes Asians better math performers. Perhaps some people think that there is a being-good-at-math gene that Asians tend to have and that others tend to lack, but this is not backed by any evidence. There are probably many complex reasons why it is true that on average East Asians score higher on math tests than students of European descent. The point is just that someone who makes use of this positive stereotype need not have any opinion at all on what those reasons are.

The second reason for thinking that the second premise is true is that it is very difficult to see how anyone could be harmed by the use of a positive stereotype. Who could be harmed? I am going to assume that it doesn't make any sense to talk about an entire group of people being harmed unless some individuals in the group are harmed. So consider the stereotype about Asians and math at the level of the individual. Is any Asian individual harmed? It's hard to see how. That individual is being told, by the person who uses the stereotype, that they are a member of a group that tends to be good at math. Where is the harm there? Is any non-Asian individual harmed? Again, it's hard to see how. That individual is being told that a certain group of people (of which they are not a member) tends to be good at math. Any non-Asian who claims to be *harmed* by the claim has a threshold for being "harmed" that is way too low.

It is important to keep in mind that although people might be *offended* by the use of stereotypes, it does not follow that they are *harmed* by the use of stereotypes. Very roughly, the difference between harm and offense is this: When someone harms you they prevent you from achieving what you want to achieve; they makes it so that you cannot get what you take to be the good stuff out of life. But when someone merely offends you, they basically just hurt your feelings. Having your feelings hurt is very different from not being able to get what you want out of life. It might be that offense can sometimes lead to harm; it might be that someone can hurt your feelings so badly that you will not be able to function as you otherwise could and would want to. This is why *negative* stereotypes are both offensive *and* harmful. But positive stereotypes, even if they might be offensive, are not harmful. Note too that while there is good reason to accept the Harm Principle, there is no good reason to accept the Offense Principle, which says that an action is morally wrong if it causes offense. In fact, there is good reason to reject the Offense Principle: It would require too much of moral agents. Just about anything I say has the potential to offend someone somewhere. You might know someone who is just a little too touchy about things. Some people tend to get terribly upset even when their friends tease them in a good-natured way. But the problem in such a situation doesn't lie with the teaser. It's the person who gets so bent out of shape who has the problem and (arguably) acts immorally. Or, to take another example, consider the teacher who gives her student a low grade on an assignment. The low grade might hurt the student's feelings, but we don't want to say that the teacher thereby does something immoral by giving the student a low grade (assuming the student really does deserve the low grade).

For the reasons just given, all of the premises of the above argument are true. It follows that the use of positive stereotypes is not always morally wrong. That is not to say that *every* time someone makes use of positive stereotypes, they are in the moral clear. It might be possible to make use of positive stereotypes in order to do real harm. If you do that, then of course you act immorally. The point is just that you do not act immorally *just* in virtue of using a positive stereotype. Positive stereotypes are not morally problematic in and of themselves.

Con

It is immoral to make use of stereotypes to describe people, even if the stereotypes do not have negative connotations. Those who think the use of positive stereotypes is morally permissible have a simplistic view of what kinds of things might or might not cause harm to people. Reality is a bit more complex than the pro side of this issue would have you think. The argument for the immorality of the use of positive stereotypes can be summarized like this:

(1) If the use of positive stereotypes causes harm, then the use of positive stereotypes is morally wrong.

(2) If the use of positive stereotypes causes people to feel less capable or unworthy, then the use of positive stereotypes causes harm.

(3) The use of positive stereotypes causes people to feel less capable and unworthy.

---

(4) The use of positive stereotypes is morally wrong.

I don't think I need to do much to convince you that the first premise is true. It might be that if there were some good reason to use positive stereotypes, and the good of their use outweighed the bad, then their use would be morally ok in some situations. But I think most people agree that using positive stereotypes is not something we need to do or even something that there is any particularly good reason to do. So, if they cause harm, we shouldn't use them. And if they cause harm, then they cause *needless* harm, and it is always wrong to cause needless harm.

The second premise is perhaps slightly more controversial than the first, but not by a lot. The point is *not* that we should equate hurt feelings and harm. Rather, the claim is that if the use of positive stereotypes causes people to feel less capable or unworthy, that *in turn* will cause them harm. This is a big reason why the use of negative stereotypes is morally unacceptable.

But why think that *positive* stereotypes are likely to make people feel less capable or unworthy? This is the claim in the third premise, and you might think that the claim is implausible. Sure, you might say, if someone negatively stereotyped me, I might thereby feel less capable, but why would I feel less capable if someone said something *good* about my race, gender, or whatever? To understand the right answer to this question, it is important that we keep in mind that stereotypes are loose generalizations. In order for a loose generalization about a group to be true, it need only be the case that it is true of a large percentage of the members of the group. In this way loose generalizations are different from generalizations that are meant to hold universally. So, something like "Dogs have four legs" is a loose generalization that is true, even though there are a few three- and two-legged dogs out there. On the other hand, the claim "Dogs are mammals" is true and it is true universally; there isn't even one dog that isn't a mammal.

But what does this have to do with the harm caused by positive stereotypes? Well, since they are loose generalizations, there will be members of the group that is stereotyped who do not have the characteristics attributed to them. So, for example, even if it is true that people of East Asian descent *tend* to perform better in a mathematical academic setting, there are, of course, many people of Asian descent who do not perform as well as other Asians or even as well as the average math student. So we need to consider the effects of positive stereotypes on *them*. If you are a member of a group that is stereotyped positively, but you think that the positive characterization isn't true of you, you are likely to think that you are less worthy—that you are less than you should be. You will lack confidence. You will think that there must be something wrong with you personally because you are a member of a group that *should* be good at something that you simply are not all that good at. You will second guess yourself as a person. These things are in turn likely to cause you harm, in that you will not be as able as you otherwise would have been to successfully pursue your goals.

The problem with positive stereotypes goes the other way too: Positive stereotypes negatively affect people who are members of the stereotyped group and who fit the stereotype. Consider the student of Asian descent who is exceptionally talented at mathematics. When they are subjected to "Asians are good at math," they are likely to think that their talent is due to their group membership and doesn't have much to do with them as an individual. They might think that there is nothing for them, *as an individual*, to be proud of. After all, the stereotype suggests that there is nothing about them, *as an individual*, that explains their mathematical talent. This situation can also cause a lack of confidence or self-assurance and hence cause harm in the long run.

Finally, the use of positive stereotypes can lead to the use of negative stereotypes, and negative stereotypes are clearly problematic. If you say "Asians are good at math," you might also be very tempted to say, "Non-Asians are not so good at math," which obviously could have bad effects for non-Asians. We have already assumed that the use of negative stereotypes is not permissible, so if the use of positive stereotypes increases the risk that people will use negative stereotypes as well, that is yet another bad consequence of positive stereotypes.

These are the ways in which positive stereotypes can and do harm people. And remember that this discussion takes place in a context where there is no obvious reason for positive stereotypes to be used in the first place. If there is no good reason to think that the use of positive stereotypes does any *good*, then the mere *possibility* that they do bad seems to be good enough reason for us to refuse to use them in dealing with our fellow humans.

To drive the point home, consider another realm in which people tend to use stereotypes, not about other humans, but rather about non-human animals. For example, dog breeders and others tend to apply stereotypes—both positive and negative—to different breeds of dog. Insofar as dog breeds are analogous to human races, the cases are analogous. But the similarity ends there. To see why, it is useful to ask why we do not think it is wrong to make use of negative stereotypes in classifying dogs. For example, why is it not obviously immoral to say that beagles are stubborn, a little on the dumb side, and hence hard to train? The pretty clear answer, I think, is that this negative stereotype, associated with beagles, is very unlikely to do any harm to any beagles. Since no beagle understands that they have been stereotyped this way, it is hard to imagine how any beagle could be adversely affected by the negative stereotype. And the same goes for positive stereotypes of dog breeds. The German shepherd who is an outlier—who is not easy to train, who is not very loyal—doesn't know that he is an outlier, and so cannot be harmed by the positive stereotypes some people associate with German shepherds. The point is just that what is relevant to the moral permissibility of the use of stereotypes has everything to do with the mindset of those being stereotyped. When it comes to dog breeds, if positive stereotypes cannot adversely affect individual dogs because the mindset of individual dogs is not affected by those stereotypes, then negative stereotypes of dog breeds can do no harm for the very same reason. Inversely, in the case of humans, if negative stereotypes adversely affect individual people because their mindset is likely to be negatively altered as a result, then positive stereotypes do harm for the very same reason.

40. Is it ever ok to speak or write derogatory names for groups, e.g., racial slurs?

Clarification

It is very important to recognize that there is a difference between *using* a term and *mentioning* a term. See the pro essay below for an explanation of the difference. The question is whether it is morally permissible to *mention* slurs by speaking or writing the slurs themselves. Presumably, educated people tend to agree that there is something wrong with *using* them. Let us restrict our question to be about slurs that are thought to be very derogatory and very powerful. We are not talking about words such as 'Yankee' or 'Canuck,' which might be thought of as slurs (kind-of) but which are not typically thought to be all that derogatory or all that powerful in and of themselves. (Note that the plural versions of both examples are the names of professional sports teams that purportedly represent the groups referred to.)

Pro

I do not like the taste of bananas. I don't expect you to care, but I do want you to notice that the first sentence of this essay *uses* the word 'bananas.' The second sentence of this essay *mentions* the word 'bananas' as does this third sentence. There is a big difference. When I use the word, what am I referring to? I'm referring to the green- or yellow-skinned, sweet and mushy fruits that grow on trees in East Asia and parts of the Americas and which I detest. When I mention the word, what am I referring to? I'm referring to the word itself—a three-syllable word that begins with the second letter of the English alphabet, has an interesting repetitive phonetic structure, and which is kinda fun to say. This use/mention distinction explains how the following is true: Brian hates bananas but loves 'bananas.' It is common for philosophers of language and logicians to write single quotes as I just did to indicate that a word is being mentioned and not used. See the difference? It's a big one. Now consider the case where an ignorant racist *uses* the n-word to insult or intimidate a Black person and compare it to the case where a professor of English literature *mentions* the n-word in class by reading aloud from a novel by James Baldwin (an acclaimed African American author whose work sometimes includes the n-word). Again, there is a big difference.

My claim is that there is absolutely nothing wrong with mentioning slurs by actually uttering or writing them. People who think that merely mentioning these words is morally wrong seem to either ignore or be unaware of the use/mention distinction. Furthermore, objecting to the mere mention of slurs leads to a harmful social situation, or so I will argue. I take it for granted that no white person should ever use the n-word. But to think that it is immoral for a white person to merely mention the word is to be confused about how language works and how the word has gained the power it has. Since the main argument that mentioning slurs is immoral seems to rely on a false premise, I reject the argument. Since there doesn't seem to be any other argument forthcoming, I don't see how or why we should think that merely mentioning-by-uttering slurs is immoral.

You might object that there is no positive reason *for* thinking that the mentioning of a slur is a good thing. In other words, one might object that regardless of *why* people are offended by the mere mention of slurs, the fact is that they are and no benefit is gotten by mentioning them. So why would you ever write or say a slur anyway?

The answer to this objection is that mentioning particular slurs by actually speaking or writing them can serve an important goal. Or, at least, mentioning slurs can help to prevent a bad result. Specifically, that bad result is that an outright refusal to utter or write slurs in public discourse infantilizes us, and we shouldn't treat ourselves or others that way. For example, it would be newsworthy (to say the least) if a public official in the United States were to *use* the n-word. So how should media outlets report this news? How should people tell others about what the politician said? It seems they have three options:

(1) 'Politician X used a racial slur.'
(2) 'Politician X said the n-word.'
(3) 'Politician X said [insert the full word here]'

Option (1) or anything like it doesn't even really indicate what was said. Anybody who hears (1) is going to immediately ask, "WHAT racial slur did they use?" And the answer might matter. Some slurs are worse than others and whether X used a slur that refers to their own group might be an important consideration too. Are we so delicate that we can't even be told what X actually said?

Option (2) is also bad. Everyone who hears anything like (2) knows full well what the n-word in question is. Nobody is going to think that maybe Politician X used the word 'nincompoop.' If everybody knows what the n-word is and will automatically say the full word to themselves, then what purpose is served by using this 'n-word' language? The situation in (2) is similar to an adult who, for some reason, thinks they should not use 'hell' as an expletive but weirdly thinks that it is acceptable to say 'H-E-double hockey sticks.' It's just childish. And you don't have to be a professional reporter or newscaster to either contribute to an infantile atmosphere of discourse by talking as in (1) or (2) or to act like an adult concerned about serious issues by talking as in (3).

Con

If the author of the pro essay *really* thinks that it is ok to mention particularly abhorrent slurs, then why doesn't he do so? The pro essay mentions the 'n-word,' but never mentions the full word. Why? Because the word is a prohibited word, and because it should be prohibited, and because the author understands all of this.

The pro essay tries to make a lot out of the use/mention distinction. But the use/mention distinction is not enough to overcome the fairly obvious moral drawbacks of uttering or writing slurs. It is true that there is a linguistic and semantic distinction between using a word and mentioning it. It is also true that there is a big moral difference between using a slur and mentioning it. It just doesn't follow, however, that it is acceptable to mention a slur by uttering or writing it. Pretty obviously there can be a moral distinction between two things and for both of them to be wrong. There is a big difference between murdering your neighbor and stealing their garden rake, but it's still wrong to steal their rake.

There is something wrong—perhaps many things wrong—with *using* a racial slur. I will not try to list all those things here. I invite readers to come up with their own list. The main point is just that whatever considerations make us think that using slurs is wrong, they also make any uttering or writing of them wrong, even if mentioning is not as bad as using. There is a moral residue in mentioning-by-saying a slur left over from using a slur. This means that mentioning-by-saying inherits some of the wrongness of using.

To make this point clearer, let's consider other cases of moral residue. For example, why is it that most respectable media outlets do not show video of beheadings carried out by terrorists or publish grisly photos of murder victims? There are a lot of possible and plausible answers to this question, but for present purposes the important point is that although showing or publishing beheadings or the bodies of murdered people is obviously not as bad as beheading or murdering, there is still something wrong with the showing or publishing. The badness of the initial act seems to infect the broadcasting of the disgusting details of the act. Likewise, the badness of using a slur seems to infect any instance in which someone says it, even if they say it only to mention it. This similarity explains what is wrong with mentioning slurs. Whatever bad things are associated with using a slur are also associated with mentioning it.

It is not very often that you need to know that someone has used a slur. But if such a situation should arise, it is easy enough to mention a specific slur without speaking or writing it. Note that the phrase 'n-word' is now a common way to *mention* the racial slur. Note too that this convention works well enough. Just as we don't need to be subjected to all of the details of terrorists beheading someone in order to know what the terrorists have done, we don't have to hear a slur spoken or read a slur written in order to know that someone used a slur. To suggest, as the pro essay does, that a refusal to utter or write slurs is childish is very similar to suggesting that it is childish to refuse to watch a video of a beheading. Furthermore, it seems that whatever motivates the claim that it is childish to refuse to utter or write slurs also motivates the claim that it is childish to refuse to watch a gruesome beheading. We know, however, that it is *not* childish to refuse to watch a gruesome beheading. If anything, that is precisely what a virtuous adult would do. Similarly, a virtuous adult does not utter or write a slur, even if they "just" want to mention it.

Option 3—It depends. Be careful!

In certain circumstances, *mentioning* racial slurs might be permissible. One such circumstance is the example used above—quoting directly from a great piece of literature in which a slur appears. But you have to be *very careful*. Racial and gendered slurs such as the n-word and the c-word are so infused with a history of racism and sexism that to even mention them one stands a good chance of offending people, or making them very angry, even when they fully understand the use/mention distinction. And what do you really achieve by actually saying the full word anyway? The con essay gets this much right: Usually, you should say something like 'n-word' instead. Everyone will know what word you're talking about, and nobody will be offended or angry. And no, it's not infantile like 'H-E-double hockey sticks.'

Ask yourself what your real motives are in mentioning a slur by actually saying or writing the full slur. Are they good motives? Or maybe you're a little bit of a bigot? Or maybe you just enjoy breaking taboos? Or maybe you want to show that you can say whatever you damn-well please, and fuck anyone who doesn't like it? But if you're *sure* that your motives are good, and the context is right, and that everyone will understand and accept what you're doing, and that your tone of voice is appropriate (or your writing includes quotation marks around the slur) and that you first flag the necessity of your mention and assure your audience that no harm is intended, then, well, maybe, er, um, ... go ahead.

About the Publisher

The word "broadview" expresses a good deal of the philosophy behind our company. Our focus is very much on the humanities and social sciences—especially literature, writing, and philosophy—but within these fields we are open to a broad range of academic approaches and political viewpoints. We strive in particular to produce high-quality, pedagogically useful books for higher education classrooms—anthologies, editions, sourcebooks, surveys of particular academic fields and sub-fields, and also course texts for subjects such as composition, business communication, and critical thinking. We welcome the perspectives of authors from marginalized and underrepresented groups, and we have a strong commitment to the environment. We publish English-language works and translations from many parts of the world, and our books are available world-wide; we also publish a select list of titles with a specifically Canadian emphasis.

broadview press

This book is made of paper from well-managed FSC® - certified
forests, recycled materials, and other controlled sources.